CHRIST CENTERED FINANCES

Your Money Matters

Bill Yeomans

Christ Centered Finances
Your Money Matters

Editor: Marelene P. Yeomans

Cover by: SelfPubBookCovers/GoodCoverDesign

ISBN -13:9781518695230
ISBN-10:151869523X
William Yeomans
P O Box 2088
Fort Bragg, CA 95437
william.yeomans.fb@gmail.com

ABOUT THE AUTHOR

Pastor Bill Yeomans writes from many years of experience in the world of finance. He has been responsible for forming Church budgets for over forty years. He then was tasked with leading Church Finance Committees and teaching them to live within those same budgets. He has served as Development Officer to a Christian Non Profit Corporation, raising Millions of Dollars each year. He has served as Assistant Security Officer of the United States Naval War College and as Division Officer aboard The Aircraft Carrier USS Ranger during the Vietnam War.

The author holds a M.S. in Education and a M. Div. from Golden Gate Baptist Theological Seminary. After release from active duty, he taught Eighth Grade Mathematics in California. He has also taught numerous financial seminars. He is an entrepreneur and has started. and subsequently sold several businesses. He and his wife have lived a debt-free lifestyle for many years. He learned the joy of tithing at least 10% of his income from his Father-in-Law who put God first while raising six children on the pay of a school principal.

Pastor Bill and his wife Marelene have six grown children and ten grandchildren. They have been married for fifty-three years and make their home on the Pacific Coast of Northern California with their Rottweiler dog named Jasmine. Jasmine means "Loved of God"

DEDICATION

This book is dedicated to the men and women
Who have proved faithful to God
In giving to Him their lives and their fortunes
To build His Church here on Earth

CONTENTS

FOREWARD

Welcome to the wide wonderful world of finances! The concept of managing your finances can be both frightening and exhilarating at the same time. It is almost like learning to ski. Try to imagine the first time you arrive at the ski mountain and look at the beginner slope. Your heart begins to pound and the adrenalin starts to flow just a wee bit faster. You notice many children and some adults having varying degrees of success or failure, depending on your own perspective. As you stand there watching, you notice how nearly everyone seems to be falling down. Again and again, over and over, down they go. As you watch, an interesting fact comes to your attention. The children fall down and get back up laughing and having fun. It seems they laugh with increasing delight as they fall down over and over again. Then as you stand there watching, these laughing children are falling down less and less often and are skiing further and further between falls. But they are still laughing! These kids are having fun learning how to become skilled skiers. You feel quite certain that by the end of the first day, many of them will graduate from the beginner's slope to the next level of proficiency.

Then you begin to study the small handful of adults who are also trying out their skill on the beginners' slope. These grownups are falling down with the same frequency as the children, but there seems to be something different happening. They don't appear to be laughing quite the same way as the children. They act like every fall is a tiny embarrassment. These adults will probably succeed at becoming accomplished skiers with some effort. What is the difference? Why will most kids progress much faster than their parents or other adults? PERCEPTION! If you think it will be fun, then it most likely will be fun. If you are fearful you will make mistakes, then it will probably be a whole lot less enjoyable.

The same principle holds true when learning a foreign language. Children just start talking and expect to be understood. Adults don't begin talking until they know they will speak correctly in order to be understood. To many adults, making a mistake spells failure. With a child, simply being understood is a total victory!

Without being overly simplistic, I can say that the field of finance is similar in many ways to the illustrations of learning to ski or learning another language. Assuming that you can add and subtract with a fair amount of confidence, you can learn to successfully manage your finances. It helps to understand that little mistakes can become learning tools that will prevent making more serious mistakes when the stakes are higher, or later, when the 'Steaks' become more affordable! (Pun intended!)

PRESUMPTION: The reader is a believer in Godly principles and seeks to please God with his or her actions. This book is not a get-rich scheme nor is it an attempt to sell or influence the reader to purchase any financial plan or product.

This book is written from a Christian perspective. The author makes no apology for his Biblical approach to financial matters. The author makes no attempt to persuade the reader to accept any religious perspective except as it pertains to wise financial decisions. God has to come first, at all times and especially in tough times. Before we look at the powerful influence of how money matters in most of our lives, it may help to take a careful look at some of the significant ways Scripture addresses the subject. Okay, are we ready to begin?

SECTION ONE

Teaching Of Scripture

CHAPTER 1
PUTTING GOD FIRST

"Honor the Lord with your wealth and with the best part of everything you produce" (Prov.3:9). Notice the writer stresses the fact that we are to honor God in every financial transaction. We show honor to God by presenting him with the very best part of whatever it is we are able to bring before him as our offering.

"What can we bring to the Lord? Should we bring him burnt offerings? Should we bow before God most high with offerings of yearling calves? Should we offer him thousands of rams and ten thousand rivers of olive oil? Should we sacrifice our firstborn children to pay for our sins? No, O people, the Lord has told you what is good, and this is what he requires of you: *to do what is right, to love mercy*, and *to walk humbly with your God*" (Micah 7:6-8).

Here the Scripture develops the desires of God into another dimension. He transcends the physical acts of giving to concentrate on the Spiritual realm of giving to God what he really desires. Our ability to please God completely involves our willingness to change our personal values to correspond with the person and the purpose of God. First and foremost, God requires us to *do what is right* all of the time and at all costs. This seems to be a rather tall order you may be thinking. Remember this is the desire of our loving God to make our lives count for him and his kingdom here on earth. It may seem easy to justify what we do as being the right thing in a particular circumstance, but does this meet God's requirement? He wants us to be doers of what is truly right at all times. There are no exceptions!

Secondly, God requires us *to love mercy*. This goes hand in hand with the requirement to do what is right every time. To love mercy involves a heart decision combined with a head decision. The natural inclination of sinful man is to be judgmental. To feel that the sinner 'gets what he or she deserves'. That is not the way God chooses to work. God chooses to be merciful because of the sacrifice of his Son, Jesus who died on that Roman Cross to gain our pardon from sin. The entire purpose of God was to reconcile sinful man to a loving Father. That takes Grace. God's underserved favor being poured out upon us in order to restore fellowship with him. This is why God requires each believing, born-again Christian to literally *love to have mercy* toward each other. Many people substitute the word 'love' with the phrase 'am willing to'. It is so much easier to 'be willing to' show mercy than it is to 'love to have' mercy! God is asking for a change in my heart condition toward my fellow man.

Thirdly, God requires us *to walk humbly with our God*. The awesome fact that God invites us to walk with him, should be more than enough to make us feel humble! Sadly, many self-described Christians have tremendous problems with pride. Many seem to feel that they are among the privileged few who have been chosen to walk with God. God requires just the opposite from his people. He wishes us to walk with him with the greatest humility. Knowing that none of us are, or ever will be, worthy to walk with our Holy God. God requires us t*o walk humbly with our God,* so that the whole world will understand how loving and forgiving he truly has been toward his chosen ones.

"Should people cheat God? Yet you have cheated me! But you ask, 'What do you mean? When did we ever cheat you?' You have cheated me of the tithes and offerings due to me. You are under a curse, for your whole nation has been cheating me. Bring all the tithes into the storehouse so there will be enough food in my temple. If you do, says the Lord of heaven's Armies, I will open the windows of heaven for you. I will pour out a blessing so great you won't have enough room to take it in! Try it! Put me to the test!" (Malachi 3:8-12).

People will never joyfully give a tithe (Tenth) of their income to God unless they have had a genuine heart transformation. When this happens, Believers will gladly pour out their financial blessings to support God's ministries. When a twice-born believer comes into the very presence of the living God, he or she is utterly overwhelmed with the love of God that has been shed upon their life. When the floodgates of God's love are poured out upon a believer, the most natural reaction is to do everything in their power to bless others in the same way. Only a hardness of the heart can cause a stinginess of the purse. David the shepherd lad cries out to God, "May the words of my mouth and the meditation of my heart be pleasing to you, O Lord, my rock and my redeemer" (Psalm 19:14). He is telling God that he wants to please his Lord with his words and all of his being. Here David displays total devotion to God.

Personal examples of changed hearts.

ZACCHAEUS: A chief tax collector of Jericho, and he was wealthy.

"Jesus entered Jericho and made his way through the town. There was a man there named Zacchaeus. He was one of the most influential Jews in the Roman tax collecting business, and he had become very rich. He tried to get a look at Jesus, but he was too short to see over the crowds. So he ran ahead and climbed a Sycamore-fig tree beside the road, so he could watch from there, for Jesus was going to pass that way. When Jesus came by, he looked up at Zacchaeus and called him by name. 'Zacchaeus!' he said, 'quick, come down! I must be a guest in your home today.' Zacchaeus quickly climbed down and took Jesus to his house in great excitement and joy. But the people were displeased. 'He has gone to be the guest of a notorious sinner,' they grumbled. Meanwhile Zacchaeus stood before the Lord and said, 'Lord I will give away half my wealth to the poor, Lord, and if I have cheated people on their taxes, I will give them back four times as much'" (Luke 19:1-8).

Here we have a true example of a man who was changed when he had a meeting with Jesus. His heart was changed which led to a complete change in how he valued his accumulated wealth. He immediately gave half (50%) of all that he had, to help the poor. He also pledged to undo all his previous acts of dishonesty. He promised to make right any acts of dishonesty by repaying back four times as much as he had taken. (400%). This was an act unheard of! Here was a man who had honestly had a spiritual conversion. Jesus made this public announcement, "Salvation has come to this home today, for this man has shown himself to be a son of Abraham. And I, the Son of Man, have come to seek and to save those like him who are lost" (Luke 19:9-10).

Scripture identifies another tax collector who was challenged by Jesus. Jesus asked a tax collector named Levi, (also known as Matthew) to be one of his original disciples. This is recorded in two of the Gospel accounts. "As he walked along, he saw Levi son of Alphaeus sitting at his tax-collection booth. 'Come, be my disciple,' Jesus said to him. So Levi got up and followed him" (Mark 2:14). and (Matthew 9:9). Here we have another example in Scripture of how Jesus was, and still is, willing to use any person, who has had a true heart conversion. This can be a man or woman. A tax collector or a religious leader. A housewife or a college student. Social position doesn't matter to Jesus. He always looks at one's heart condition. "Wherever your treasure is, there your heart and thoughts will also be" (Matthew 6:21).

CHAPTER 1 JOURNAL

PUTTING GOD FIRST

Can you remember any time where you did not put God first?

Have you gone to God in prayer and asked for his forgiveness?

Have you done whatever possible to make this right?

Have you knowingly cheated others?

Is it possible to make this right? If so, will you do it?

CHAPTER 2

HONESTY

"The Lord despises double standards of all kinds" (Proverbs 20:10). To 'despise' also means to hate or loathe or detest or abhor. How terrible to realize that God despises something a person could be tempted to do. Double standards might be as simple as charging different prices for the same goods or services. Double standards could be using one's influence or perceived power to gain an unfair advantage in some financial transaction. Double standards might be seen as seeking unfair tax advantages not open to everyone. The list could continue, but I'm sure you understand the concept. Scripture never suggests that a little cheating is permitted as long as it goes undetected. The Word of God states that the lord *detests* any such actions. Remember that God knows everything about you, nothing is hidden from God.

The book of Proverbs adds another concept of dishonesty. "Don't steal your neighbor's property by moving the ancient boundary markers..." (Proverbs 22:28). This Scripture expands on the Ten Commandments handed down to Moses by God. "You shall not steal… you shall not covet anything that is your neighbor's" (Exodus 20:15-17).

God empowered Moses to travel back into Egypt to be the man God chose to lead the Hebrew slaves out of Egypt and into the 'Promised Land'. These people had endured horrible cruelty under their Egyptian taskmasters for a period of four hundred years. They existed by following the rules of these Egyptians. They had no concept of fairness or any other rules of this new God who Moses told them about. Because of this, Moses was called by God to climb a mountain and meet with God to receive ten commandments written in two stone tablets. These were divided into their responsibilities toward God and toward their fellow man. Jesus paraphrased these into two statements. He told us to Love God and to love our fellow man.

Lying is another form of dishonesty "Wealth created by a lying tongue is a vanishing mist and a deadly trap" (Prov.21:6). Put simply, God hates liars. Jesus called Satan the Father of Liars. This verse teaches that any ill-gotten wealth gained by lies and deception will not last. Such deception is void of any wisdom needed to make it last. Even more important is the fact that any and all lies are an abomination to God. God is the very essence of truth. Satan is the embodiment of all that is false. Therefore, Scripture warns that if we become liars in the way we conduct our business, then by default, we place ourselves under the control of the enemy. This act then becomes a deadly trap for our souls.

"Income from charging high interest rates will end up in the pocket of someone who is kind to the poor" (Prov.28:8). You cannot take it with you. Such ill-gotten interest takes money from the poor. This is stealing from them. There is no other explanation for this corruption. God says that such profit will be inherited by one who will be kind and honest toward the people who need it the most.

"Better to be poor and honest than to be dishonest and rich" (Prov.28:6). God places the highest praise on all who are totally honest. There are many ways to be truly rich. Accumulating money <u>is not</u> one of them. Honesty always pleases God. "Choose a good reputation over great riches..." (Prov.22:1). A good reputation is also a good witness for the Lord. "Better to have little with godliness, than to be rich and dishonest" (Prov.16:8). Quite frankly, I enjoy a hamburger much better than steak. "The Lord demands accurate scales and balances; he set the standards for fairness" (Prov.16:11).

Here we have overwhelming evidence that God demands complete honesty from his people when dealing with the public and with each other. Our Christian testimony depends on our reputation of dealing with complete honesty and integrity at all times. If all people will live by these standards many lawyers will need to cross-train for another line of work! Scripture teaches us to be men and women of our word.

CHAPTER 2 JOURNAL

HONESTY

Are there times when you have knowingly cheated someone?

If so, have you confessed this to God?

If possible, have you made this right with the person or persons?

Are you willing to make this happen?

CHAPTER 3
TAKING CHANCES

The temptation to gamble comes from a strong desire to get something for nothing. There is, and always has been, the mentality that we deserve so many benefits that we haven't worked for. One can feel lucky and want just one more roll of the dice or one more hand of poker to be a winner. Many gamblers are driven by the idea they just know they are about to win in a big way. They know that their 'ship is about to come in'. They know that the rotating wheel will stop on their number. They are truly believing their horse will win the next race. They simply know their favorite sports team will win this game, or will become the Super-bowl champs! This sickness can become all consuming. Even to the point of betting their kid's lunch money on who will be the next Heavyweight Champ of the World! Since the beginning of time, men and women have been captivated with the desire to win! The Grand Prix or the office pool, it really doesn't matter. In the book of Proverbs, we are told, "Trust in your money, and down you go!" (Proverbs 11:28a). "Those who bring trouble on their families inherit only the wind. The fool will be servant to the wise" (Proverbs 11:29). "Wealth from get-rich-quick schemes quickly disappears; wealth from hard work grows" (Proverbs 13:11). "We may throw the dice, but the Lord determines how they fall" (Proverbs 16:33). These verses, along with others, would seem to indicate a strong negative approach to gambling found in Scripture.

Perhaps there is nothing wrong with a friendly, small wager on a sporting event. However, the desire to win can quickly take control of all common sense. There are local chapters of Gamblers Anonymous in many cities that are a grim reminder of the dangers to be found. When this becomes a problem and controls your financial decisions, it is time to do a careful self-evaluation. Many families suffer financial ruin when gambling becomes a driving force for one or both parents. A basketball star who earned millions of dollars each year had to declare personal bankruptcy. This in turn led to a tragic divorce due to his addiction to gambling. A college student lost his tuition funds and had to drop out of college. Poker became too much of a temptation. He just knew he could beat the odds. It would seem he had never considered taking a class in 'Statistical Probability'. More people lose than win! This is an absolute fact. The profit that is gained by gambling is a major source of revenue for States and Native American Reservations that permit it. Why is this possible? The simple fact is that many more people lose than win! If one simply needs to have their weekly poker game, try using pebbles or hard candy for your monetary rewards. This way nobody gets hurt or feels cheated.

CHAPTER 3 JOURNAL

TAKING CHANCES

Are you now a gambler?

Have you ever been one?

Has this, or is this now causing problems?

Are you willing to take steps to stop the habit?

If yes, what steps are you willing to take?

SECTION TWO

Controlling Your Money

CHAPTER 4
LEARNING CONTROL

What place does money have in your life? Does money control you or do you control your money? A person may wonder what in the world does the author mean? Perhaps we need to use a small 'Litmus Test' A litmus paper is a small strip of paper which has been treated with a chemical so that when it comes in contact with a particular substance, it turns a certain specified color. Let's use a money litmus paper that will turn green every time the answer to a question about personal finances has a negative response. Let's begin. Do you have money left over at the end of each month? At the end of each month, do you have unpaid credit cards? Do you have to closely watch your bank balance in order not to become overdrawn? Are you ever late making regular monthly payments? Do you know your current credit score? Do you at times have to choose which bills to pay due to limited account balances? Do you and your spouse ever argue over money? Do you ever 'bounce' a check due to insufficient funds? Does your car payment seem too high? Have you considered ways to lower these payments? Does it seem as if your bills grow bigger over time? Do you only pay the 'minimum due' on credit cards or time payments? Do you have more than two credit cards? Do you have a savings account? Do you have one or more retirement accounts? Do you love to shop till you drop? Does worry about finances trouble your sleep? Do you think this exercise is 'stupid'?

If you found your litmus test strip turning green more often than not, then it is fair to suggest that money controls many of your financial decisions. If you know that you have complete victory and control over the items in your litmus test, you need to be congratulated! You need to jump up and down and loudly shout to the world "I am completely in control of every aspect of my finances." However, if you are like over 90% of all families, you will need to take a more somber approach to your finances. Chapter five is going to provide a calculated approach to how you can become in charge of your financial decisions beginning right now. This is called forming a family budget that is formed by you, exclusively for your family situation. The main reason that many folks don't like the concept of a budget is that quite often budgets don't seem to work. Much like many diets, they are too restrictive and offer few rewards. But what if you could design a diet, or a budget, that was totally yours. Your design and yours to change and modify as you went along. Does this approach sound more likely to allay your fears and to offer a better chance of success? Let's give it a try.

CHAPTER 4 JOURNAL

LEARNING CONTROL

Are you totally in control of your finances?

Or do you identify with the 90% factor?

Are you and your family currently operating within a family budget?

If not, are you willing to give it a try?

If your answer is no, perhaps you need to skip Chapter 5 at least for the present.

CHAPTER 5

FORMING A BUDGET

Why does the average person or family need to formulate a budget? There may be several answers to this question. For a significant group of persons, regulating how the money comes and goes, simply seems like an exercise in futility. Who knows or who even cares as long as everything works out somehow, and every so often. Budgeting money seems like such a drag. It is a boring exercise with very little upside and considerable downside. For many families the concept of a budget just adds another level of control that seems to seldom work as intended. Therefore, the terms of 'Budget' and 'Frustration' simply stated just add up to more stress added to an already stressful family dynamic. In open rebellion many will misquote Scripture by claiming "The Bible says that money is the root of all that is evil". Let me explain that this is <u>NOT</u> what the Bible states. Scripture simply states that the <u>love</u> of money, the <u>lusting</u> after money, leads to all that is evil.

WRITING YOUR OWN BUDGET

Why does it need to be in writing? Many of you will relate with this author when it comes to having a somewhat sketchy memory at best. The longer we live, the shorter our memory seems to get. With this in mind, it only makes sense to put your thoughts and your plans in some form of writing. A written budget proposal is far more workable and it is much easier to change and upgrade as time goes by. No budget should be ironclad. None should be written in stone. (Only the Ten Commandments were cut into stone!) When you write your own budget it still remains your own! You made it and you can change it in any way you wish. Your written budget is merely your tool to help you manage your finances in a way that makes sense to you and you alone. Because it is yours and yours alone, it need not adhere to any particular form or logic. Create your budget so that it works for you and your family situation.

HOW TO MAKE IT FLEXABLE

Do you still own a pencil? If not, go out and buy a packet of about a dozen. They are cheap. They are easy to use. They write in a format that can be EASILY ERASED! All of your budget entries and figures should be written in pencil. This just makes sense! Easy to write and easy to change. You may be a computer type person who cannot do any writing by hand. That's perfectly fine! Anything written on a computer can be upgraded or changed by a few simple strokes on your keyboard. A computer is almost as versatile as a pencil. That being said, this author still likes a pencil for first drafts while a budget is being created. Then you can transfer it into your final (but still changeable) version on the computer if you so wish.

This author sincerely wishes to emphasize the point that this budget is yours' and you can always tweak it to fit your changing needs today and far into your future. Never fear anything you have complete control over!

INCOME

Make a list of all forms of money inflow from all expected sources. Specify how often each source comes in for what amount. For fluctuating amounts, such as tips earned from some service jobs, estimate as accurately as possible. Use previous years records as a source. It may be wise to estimate a little on the low side just to be safe. Be sure to include any bonus or dividend you expect to receive, including the date and amount expected. Once you have arrived at an expected monthly income figure, you are ready to set up your budget of how you plan to disburse these funds.

MONTHLY ITEMS AND LONGER TERM EXPENSES

Get a lined pad and allow a separate line for each item.

Draw at least two columns up and down.

First column for Monthly Expenses; the other for Extended or Lump – Sum Payments

For example, if you have a $300 insurance payment due every quarter, budget $100 Monthly for this expense.

Handling your cash flow can be a bit more complicated than merely writing it into a budget. One way is to write a $100 check each month, putting them aside in a safe place. Then send in all three checks each quarter as the bill becomes due. That's just one way. Whatever method you choose to handle your cash flow for paying bills that do not come on a monthly basis, you must resist the urge to spend it for something else. If you don't figure out how to handle cash flow, the temptation is to overspend. One family I know has a savings account where they "Park" monthly amounts that will be needed on a yearly or semi-yearly basis. For instance, if the Property Tax is $1,800 per year, they place $150 each month into their savings account. Then when the tax bill arrives on the First of January, they simply withdraw the funds from their savings account and pay the bill. This is a simple, but very effective way, to handle cash flow for large bills that come infrequently. You may choose another method such as each month putting the funds in an old shoe box. Caution, don't give in to the temptation to reach into your shoe box when you feel the urge to buy two or three pairs of new shoes! You cannot wear those new shoes while confined in the County Jail!

Following is an *example* of how you may wish to start your planning process while setting up your Personal or Family Budget.

MY/OUR PRACTICE BUDGET

INCOME ESTIMATES During this example we will be using the 2014 average family income in the USA of $52,000 a year.

. Your budget can be set up in $ (Dollars) or you may choose to use % (Percentages). Either way works! I like to use percentages since for me these are much easier to adjust than dollars. It may not seem as drastic to lower 1 % than it may seem to cut dollars.

NECESSARY & RECURRING ITEMS

Tithing * 10% of 52,000 = $5,200 yr. divided by 12 = $433 month

*A significant percentage of Christian households do not Tithe!

Savings 5% of 52,000 = $2,600 yr. divided by 12 = $216 month

Housing 25% of 52,000 = $13,000 yr. divided by 12 = $1,083 month

Utilities 6% of 52,000 = $3,120 yr. divided by 12 = $260 month

Insurance 3% of 52,000 = $1,560 yr. divided by 12 = $130 a month

Transportation 9% of 52,000 = $4,680 yr. divided by 12 = $390 month

(Purchase or Lease of Auto (s) 4% (each) = $2,080 Yr. = $173 month)

(Repairs, Maintenance, Fuel, Insurance 5% = $2,600 yr.=$216 month)

Food 23% of $52,000 = $11,960yr. = $996 month = $232 week

Clothing 4% of $52,000 = $2,080 yr. = $173 month

Entertainment 5% of $52,000 = $2,600 yr. = $216 month

Miscellaneous 8% of $52,000 = $5,200 yr. = $433 month

[All credit purchases should be paid out of Miscellaneous Funds]

Emergency Fund 2% of 52,000 = $1,400 yr. = $116 month

TOTAL = 100% of $52,000 That wasn't so hard, was it?

None of these categories should be fixed in stone! Give yourself some "Wiggle Room", a little flexibility is important. Remember that your budget is your guide not your master! Conversely, it is important to strive to live within your budget as much as possible. I mean, golly gee, what's the purpose of having a budget if you are constantly finding reasons not to follow it?

How much Debt is acceptable? Go to Chapter 16 and find out!

CHAPTER 5 JOURNAL

FORMING A BUDGET

Do you agree with the concept of forming a budget?

Do you feel intimidated?

Is your spouse willing to help in this area?

If not, are you willing to take the lead?

Are you willing to swallow your pride and ask for help? Who will you ask?

Are you feeling overwhelmed?

CHAPTER 6
FOLLOWING A BUDGET

Any 'Discipline' in life requires a personal sense of discipline if it is to be successfully followed and achieved. Your budget is nothing more or nothing less than an exercise in personal discipline. It is your promise to yourself and the members of your family that you value the peace and prosperity that comes when a family has a disciplined approach to finances. Neither peace nor prosperity will be present in any family that does not follow some form of a disciplined approach to their finances. When family finances are in disarray, unhealthy family dynamics soon follow. Satan loves to use money problems as the catalyst for family problems!

Your family budget is similar to the playbook of a football team. The head coach makes up the various plays with input from the coaching staff and senior players. Then these plays are tried out on the practice field. Good plays, ones that work, are then written down in the coach's play book for use in future games. The Quarterback is expected to either memorize each play in the coach's playbook, or he must have them written down on a miniature device attached to his wrist. Then each team member is expected to know their own role or assigned task for every play in the coach's playbook. This, in essence, is how a family budget will be most successful. Your family budget works best when it becomes a team effort. Parents and more mature children who work together to make the budget work, will share in the family unity and will understand the family financial dynamics. How wonderful to have a family who each understands the inner workings of the financial decisions that are continually being made. How neat for older children to have a role in deciding financial choices. This author believes that a great deal of family stress can be avoided when finances are understood and adhered to. Again let me stress that the highest incidence of problematic marriages comes from a misunderstanding of the financial world of each person in the marriage. When everyone understands what we can and cannot afford as a family, fighting seems to just disappear.

CHAPTER 6 JOURNAL

FOLLOWING A BUDGET

Do you have a personal sense of self-discipline?

Are you willing to develop one?

Will you become the helper or the antagonist?

Why?

SECTION THREE

Loving Money

CHAPTER 7
HOARDING MONEY

Scripture is filled with lessons about storing up earthly wealth. Jesus was constantly asked questions by his enemies hoping to gain some advantage. In the Gospel of Luke, he was asked by a rich young man to be the executor of the father's estate. "Then someone called from the crowd 'Teacher, please tell my brother to divide our father's estate with me.' Jesus replied, Friend, who made me a judge over you to decide such things as that? Beware, don't be greedy for what you don't have. Real life is not measured by how much we own" (Luke 12:13-15). Jesus is speaking plainly to this man and indirectly to his brother. First of all, he is teaching against being greedy for those things belonging to others. Secondly Jesus is teaching all believers that it is wrong to suggest that God ever plays favoritism with anyone. Still another lesson being taught was that if the law of the land is definitive, it should be practiced by everyone equally. What was known by all Jewish families was the undisputed custom that upon the death of the father, his oldest son inherited twice as much as any other heirs. The remainder of the estate was to be divided equally between all other sons. It seems that the man asking Jesus to intervene was not the oldest brother. Most likely he was asking Christ to play favorites while also disrupting the age old custom.

Jesus often used a parable (story) to teach a deeper truth. One reason for this was the lack of written records or books. A good story would be likely to be remembered. He saw this as another teaching point. "And he gave an illustration: A rich man had a fertile farm that produced fine crops. In fact, his barns were full to overflowing. So he said, I know, I'll tear down my barns and build bigger ones. Then I'll have room enough to store everything. And I'll sit back and say to myself, my friend, you have enough stored away for years to come. Now take it easy, eat, drink, and be merry. But God said to him, You Fool! You will die this very night. Then who will get it all? Yes, a person is a fool to store up earthly wealth but not have a rich relationship with God" (Luke 12:16-21). If we stop and think, we may know of several people who are very wealthy in the eyes of the world, but are unhappy and even miserable. Hoarding money can produce paranoia, fear and even ulcers. It may also produce enemies.

A typical family who is very wealthy might have serious worries about protecting and safeguarding their wealth. Looking at their home we might expect to find high fences along with security gates that only opened when the security code was entered into a computer lock. You might expect to see security personnel and perhaps guard dogs. You would not be surprised to encounter financial advisors, tax lawyers and perhaps even offshore accounts. All this to protect their concept of amassing more wealth. Hoarding more wealth than they could ever hope to spend in one lifetime. They might be constantly worried about the effect of inflation or devaluation of the countries money supply. They might worry about family members being held for ransom. So much worry and so little joy! What could possibly be the point?

Two verses in Scripture come to mind. “Don’t store up treasures here on earth, where they can be eaten by moths and get rusty, and where thieves break in and steal. Store up your treasures in heaven, where they will never become moth-eaten or rusty, and where they will be safe from thieves. Wherever your treasure is, there your heart and thoughts will also be” (Matthew 6:19-21). Another verse, in the book of Proverbs states, “The rich can pay a ransom but the poor won’t even get threatened” (Proverbs 12:8).

CHAPTER 7 JOURNAL

HOARDING MONEY

Jesus also gives examples of storing up money here on earth. "What will a man give in exchange for his soul" (Matt 6:33)? "Sell all you have & come follow me" (Matthew 19:16-24).

In your opinion why do people hoard certain valuables?

Do you have the habit of hiding some of your resources?

If yes, why do you do this?

Does your marriage partner know where these exist?

Do you really trust God to provide <u>all</u> of your needs? Give yourself an example.

CHAPTER 8

LETTING GO OF MONEY'S GRIP

One of the most troublesome trends in finances is the fatal attraction of monetary wealth to a sense of security. These two concepts are separated by a wide cavern of fear and doubt. Money held in abundance does not add up to any type of security. Financial wealth often lends itself to a severe sense of insecurity. In financial circles there are two forms of perceived wealth. There is the 'Established' group of wealthy families often referred to as those with 'old money'. These are the well-known names in both business and politics that have been associated with wealth and power for centuries. Names like Rockefeller and Kellogg, resonate as household names that are instantly identified with great wealth. The list of wealthy political forces is well recognized by the average person in the United States as well as in many of the democracies and monarchies of the world. Many would agree that wealth is closely aligned with power.

Why does great wealth <u>not</u> resonate with the concept of great security? There is a saying that 'The rich get richer while the poor get poorer'. As with many such sayings, there is a certain ring of authenticity to this saying as well. It is precisely this fact that leads to a sense of foreboding among the very rich. It seems obvious that the rich are afraid of losing their money and their power that goes with it, to those who have very little. History supports the rational of this fear when we take a look at the history of revolts and resurrections against repressive leadership worldwide. Why is this author stressing this point? What does this have to do with the average person who is reading this book? If you had the few dollars to purchase this, or any other book, you have a certain amount of extra money. Buying a book or going to a show is considered discretionary spending. Please stop for a moment and give thanks that you do not have to live from week to week just trying to survive. That you don't have to live merely trying to feed yourself and your family, not certain where the money for your most basic needs will come from. Most of you, my readers, are truly rich when compared to the huge number of families that are struggling on the edge of genuine poverty.

You, my friend, are wealthy! You may choose to agree or not, but the truth is that you are among those who are blessed financially. The question is, will you strive to hold on to your wealth at any cost? Collecting wealth is like trying to pick up sand on the beach with your hands. You may hold on to a little, but the biggest portion will slip through the fingers and return to the beach. Scripture tells of a rich ruler who approached Jesus with one question that led to a more profound answer than he was expecting. "Once a religious leader asked Jesus this question: Good teacher, what must I do to inherit eternal life? Why do you call me good? Jesus asked him. Only God is truly good. But as for your question, you know the commandments. Do not commit adultery. Do not murder. Do not steal. Do not testify falsely. Honor your father and mother. The man replied, I obeyed all these commandments since I was a child. There is still one thing you lack Jesus said. Sell all you have and give the money to the poor, and you will have treasure in heaven. Then come follow me. But when the man heard this he became sad because he was very rich. Jesus watched him go and then said to his disciples, how hard it is for rich people to get into the kingdom of God! It is easier for a camel to go through the eye of a needle than for a rich person to enter the kingdom of God! (Luke 18:18-25).

CHAPTER 8 JOURNAL

LETTING GO OF MONEY'S GRIP

Make a list of the things that bugged you in this chapter.

Why do you think Jesus made such a big deal about loving money?

"Don't store up treasures here on earth where they can be eaten by moths and get rusty, and where thieves break in and steal. Store your treasures in heaven, where they will never become moth-eaten or rusty and where they will be safe from thieves. Wherever your treasure is, there your heart and thoughts will also be" (Matthew 6:19-21).

What does Jesus mean in the above Scripture quotation?

SECTION FOUR

Earning Money

CHAPTER 9
HAPPY WHILE YOU EARN

No matter who you are, no matter how well you have been educated, every person who is reading this book has one or two areas in your life that bring you great satisfaction. No matter what these may be called, either spiritual gifts, or hobbies, or special interests, you have at least one if not more of these qualities. Let me challenge you to stop for a moment and think, perhaps dream, of what your special niche in life might be. Do you like to draw? Are you one of those artist – type persons? Do you like to work with your hands? Do you have fun writing? If you had your choice of any occupation what would you choose? Do you love to cook? Would you love to be a chef? How about a carpenter? Would you enjoy working with children, and if so what age children? Are you a person who loves to garden? Perhaps wood working is your joy in life. What is it that really makes you tick? Do you wish you could go back to college and get a degree? The biggest question of all, are you satisfied with what you're doing right now? If not, what is holding you back from making a change? Change that would really bring you happiness! Poll-takers want us to believe that 80% of all persons in the labor force are unhappy with the job they are doing! How about you? Are you part of the 80% percent or perhaps are you in the 20% who loves what you are doing? Let me put it this way; how can you be happy at home if you are not happy at work? If I could read your mind you might be saying, how can I possibly change my job? I don't even have a high school education! This is the only job I've ever done! Let me challenge you to brain-storm all of the jobs that you wish you could do. Then make a list of the ones that you believe to be possible for you to achieve. Next I would suggest that you go through the list and cross out any jobs you know in your heart you can never accomplish. Hopefully, you will still have a significant number of job opportunities that may be plausible for you to investigate. One of the telltale signs of a negative person is when he or she comes up with excuses of why they cannot accomplish a certain thing. Let me ask you a question, is your glass half full or is it half empty? In other words, are you a positive thinker or are you negative? I am a firm believer that we can accomplish almost anything we set out to do if we use a little bit of common sense. Obviously a lady of 75 years of age probably will not be able to become a gymnast. However, she might know enough about gymnastics to become a teacher or a coach to younger girls. She might even know enough to write a book on how older people can succeed in jobs that have traditionally been restricted to younger people. To quote Bill Yeomans, a world-famous author, "He who thinks outside the box, will never feel boxed in"

CHAPTER 9 JOURNAL

HAPPY WHILE YOU EARN

Are you stuck in a rut?

What is your real dream job?

What steps do you need to take?

When do you plan to get going?

CHAPTER 10

LEARNING WHILE EARNING

The theme in Chapter 10 is closely related to that of chapter 9. Many times it is possible to continue learning a skill at the same time that you are performing it. If you feel stuck in a dead-end job, and yet you need this job to support your family, let's take another look. Question number one, do you have a computer? If so, can you go online? One of the wonders of the modern world is called a Google search engine. If you do not have a computer, go to your local library and sign up for a period of time on one of their computers. Most libraries offer this service free of charge. Any library that has computer access also will have Internet access. In the little town I live in, the public library has six or more computers available for use for one hour at a time. The beauty of the Google search engine is that by merely typing in a word or a phrase you will instantly be exposed to several websites that can answer many questions. Take for example, you wish to find out what is required to get your license to be a child care worker. Simply go on line and type in 'child care workers' and you will find numerous sites to select that will give you all sorts of information about what is needed and where to find it. You might want to type in the words 'online courses'. Almost instantly up will pop numerous websites with information on all types of online courses both for college credit and for just plain enjoyment. You will find everything from 'welding' to 'wedding planner'. There is almost no limit to what you can discover online through Google.com.

With the information explosion available to us today there is almost no excuse to be stuck in your old job with no way out. If you want to learn more about how to advance in the job that you now hold you can do that. If you want to learn information about a different type of job you can do that. Many employers today will give special incentives if you wish to improve yourself because they know that you will become a more valuable employee. As a side note, if you are a more valuable employee you will also be able to ask for a more respectable salary. If you become highly skilled in your profession, there will be many opportunities to advance in your own company as well as to change companies.

Perhaps an illustration from my own life would be helpful here. After graduating from high school at the age of 17, I had absolutely no clue what I wanted to accomplish or who I wanted to become for the rest of my life. I took the State College Entrance Exam and was admitted to a large university. Within 1 ½ semesters I was flunking out and quite discouraged. It seems I needed an education in the 'hard-knocks' of the real world. I went to work driving truck for a fruit wholesaler for the huge sum of $1.00 per hour. After about a year I realized that I was in a dead-end situation. I applied for a job as a machinist at an aircraft engine factory. This provided a much better income and also a chance to learn a new profession. After working at this job for a year and one half I was still dissatisfied and could not imagine doing this for the rest of my life. It was time to consider going back to college and this time to become more serious about my studies. I learned from past experience, and this time chose a small college. One where the professors actually knew your name. Since I really love kids, (I always have) I decided to pursue a teaching degree. Along came the Vietnam war which exposed me to many new possibilities. The first of these was entering and graduating from Naval Officers Candidate School. After separation from active duty, I went to graduate school, imagine that? To sum up this narrative, after graduating from Seminary I was ordained as a Minister of the Gospel and pastored numerous churches for the next 45 years. All this time I was doing what I love to do, working with people, especially children.

There was just one problem, I have never been rich. While going to seminary I was married and had two children when I started, and two more by the time I finished four years later. Just for the record, families cost money. I was offered a job as a janitor which quickly developed into owning my own janitorial service while employing 10 or 12 seminary students. Early in life I had discovered I enjoy being my own boss. This job fit me well, but I certainly never envisioned running a janitorial service for the rest of my life. My first church was small and paid little, so I took a job as a teacher's aide for which I was way over-qualified. This is just to prove a point that a job is a job when you need a job. Never be too proud to work with your hands in what some people might consider to be a dead-end occupation. Since I enjoyed being my own boss and living in small towns, most of my churches were small as well. A small church usually equals a small paycheck. Over the years I have owned and operated a cemetery and also a coin-operated laundromat, among other ventures. Yes, I believe variety is indeed the spice of life.

I am now an old 'coot' three times retired and busily writing books. I hope this illustrates that we never have to be stuck in a job that we just don't like. Especially today in the modern world of computers and the Internet we have the opportunity to pursue almost any field we choose. If You don't have the proper skills or the necessary training, then get acquainted with Google. It is extremely easy to 'Google' almost anything from anywhere in the world. Training classes as well as on-the-job training can be found for almost any job requirement. If you have the desire to learn, any Internet search engine can lead you in the right direction. The entire world is involved in a learning explosion. If you still feel stuck in a dead-end job, you have only yourself to blame. I strongly suggest you get off the couch, get on the computer, and discover all the new worlds that are out there waiting just for you.

Just a word of caution, never quit your present job until you have secured one that is better. By better I mean better pay and better job satisfaction, in that order. Remember, you are never too old and never too inexperienced to learn a new job skill. And once you learn it continue to perfect it until you become as skilled as you wish to be. The greater your skill level the more opportunities may become available to you. Think how you will feel when a company calls you and invites you to come for a job interview! If you grow tired of a company you have started, why not sell it and start something else? More about this when we come to the retirement chapters.

CHAPTER 10 JOURNAL

LEARNING WHILE EARNING

Do you plan to stay in your present job?

If yes, for how long?

What are your plans for advancement?

Why not dare to plan a little!

CHAPTER 11

INSIDE OR OUTSIDE

Do you like to work inside or outside? This may sound like a foolish question, but it's about as basic as one can get. Perhaps you have never thought of this, but most of us have a specific desire to work inside or outside. If you are one of those people who are completely neutral, meaning you have no opinion about anything, you might want to prick yourself to make sure you're still alive! Seriously my friend you must have some opinion!

I want to give you a simple exercise. Find a tablet and a pencil and write a list of all the jobs you can think of that are in your inside or outside category. You should have a list of at least 50 to 75 different jobs. Next I want you to cross out those one or two or three jobs that you absolutely would not consider even if you were hungry. Now you have a list of many possibilities. Next it would be helpful for you to start numbering these jobs in order of your preference.

The next question for you to consider, do I work better alone or with someone? Am I a team player? Would I consider working for myself, or am I more comfortable working for someone else? Do I have the courage to start my own business? If yes, what new skills will I need to learn such as bookkeeping, advertising, or marketing? If I choose to work for someone else how do I go about "selling myself" or my job skills to a potential employer? I hope these questions have started to make your blood flow just a bit faster, increased your blood pressure, and created a whole new sense of excitement! You can be, in charge of your own fate. You do not need to stay in a job that is boring, dull, or totally exasperating. The only real question is, do you have the courage to step out of your comfort zone and <u>cause change</u> to happen in your life? Yes, my friend, it does take a great deal of courage and a certain amount of persistence to make any change worthwhile. Did I mention that a high percentage of employees are not satisfied in their present job? I just wanted to make sure you caught that! Why go through life discouraged and frustrated? Why stay in a job you cannot stand? Who has convinced you that you are just plain stuck? There's an old saying "pull yourself up by your own bootstraps".

Before you break out in a cold sweat or curl up in a fetal position, let's be certain that many forms of self-employment are extremely doable. For example, those of you who like to work outside might consider a landscaping business. Both men and women could become handy-persons. You could choose to specialize and become handy in only one area where you would become an expert. You could start a window washing business or begin mowing lawns. Let your mind wander and explore many other simple occupations that require little or no added skills. Remember my previous advice, do not quit your present job until you find one that pays equally well or better. One way to accomplish this is to start your own side business and work at this part time until you develop it into a good paying full-time occupation. Then you can quit your day job.

If you are one of the folks who said you like to work inside, there are also many jobs available to you as an entrepreneur. You can open a childcare center. If you don't like children, you could open a dog grooming business. If you don't like dogs, you could go to school and become a hairdresser or a barber. If you like the company of older people you might start a business of eldercare. There are also opportunities to be caregivers for persons with handicaps. Often times people develop their hobby into a profitable business. If you don't have a hobby I strongly suggest that you find one.

CHAPTER 11 JOURNAL

INSIDE OR OUTSIDE

Okay friend, are you an 'Innie' or an 'Outie'?

(And I'm not talking about your belly button!)

The older we get the more important this question becomes.

You deserve to be happy!

What changes, if any, do you plan to make? When do you plan to make these?

CHAPTER 12
WHO EARNS AND WHO SPENDS?

Who is the person that brings home most of the family income? Is that the same person who controls most of the spending? These questions need to be examined on a more or less regular basis in order to lessen the chance of conflict over finances. I cannot emphasize strongly enough that control over finances is the number one issue most couples point to when seeking help with their marriage. Let me stress again that money represents power and power represents control. It would seem that money is the constant and main denominator concerning control issues. This being the case, it seems natural for us to examine more closely how these forces interact with each other.

The concept of a single person being responsible for most of the family income is quickly becoming obsolete. In many families across the United States and other industrialized countries, there is more than one employed member. The old picture of 'dear old dad' going to work every morning while mom stays home and tends to the other parts of family life, is rapidly disappearing. A much more common picture of American life is mom and dad both working and contributing to the finances of the family. This being the case, the next question might be "who brings home the 'lions-share' of the income?" Does this dictate whose job is more important? If one person were to lose their job how would this affect the rest of the family? What adjustments would need to be made immediately and for the future? Are both sources of income equally important?

What about an adult child who is still living at home? Does he or she contribute to the family finance? If not, is this fair to everyone else? This might be acceptable if the adult child is a full-time student living at home. In all other cases the adult family member needs to accept their responsibility to contribute in a meaningful way to the family expenses. Both parents need to agree on what is fair and present their decision to the adult child. Never allow an adult child to take advantage of your good heart or your soft side! If you do, two things will happen; the adult child will not respect you and they will continue to expect to be treated like royalty! If you find yourself in this situation, quickly get together and formulate your plan. Present your unified plan to the child and stick to it, unconditionally. Failure to follow this advice is a certain recipe for increased stress in your family. If there are younger children in the family, they will certainly watch carefully and expect to be treated with an even greater sense of being privileged.

Speaking to the family that has two or more income producing members, who should be in charge of how this income is spent? Returning to our earlier premise that the word 'money' is a synonym to the words 'power' and 'control', what is the basic issue? It's like the detective who arrives late on the scene of a murder investigation. Inevitably the question will be asked, "Who's in charge here?" Once this is established everyone else falls in line and respects the authority of whoever is in charge. This becomes rather tricky in a family with multiple wage earners. The Bible teaches that the husband is to be the head of the family under normal circumstances. But what if the circumstances are not normal? What if the wife is far better suited to be in charge of the finances? What if the husband has repeatedly demonstrated a lack of consistency in his money managing abilities? What if he is just a lousy money manager? We could fill another page with "what if's". Bottom line is that the family needs to figure these things out and proceed in complete agreement. No one person can be totally in charge of the finances and expect there to be harmony in the home. Ideally the husband is the leader and the wife is the helpmate. The most important ingredient, above all else, is the presence of loving peace and harmony concerning the financial decisions. Scripture says this far better than I could.

"Love is patient and kind. Love is not jealous or boastful or proud or rude. It does not demand its own way. It is not irritable, and it keeps no record of being wronged. It does not rejoice about injustice but rejoices whenever the truth wins out. Love never gives up, never loses faith, is always hopeful, and endures through every circumstance" (1 Corinthians 13:4-7).

CHAPTER 12 JOURNAL

WHO EARNS AND WHO SPENDS?

What control issue bothers you the most?

What is your plan to solve this issue?

Is compromise part of your plan? How?

When do you plan to get started?

CHAPTER 13

WAYS TO GENERATE MONEY

WORKING FOR SOMEON ELSE

Working as an employee is by far the most popular method of earning a living. Statistics indicate that most jobs created in the United States are from small companies and individual proprietorships. Corporate America accounts for another large section of the workforce. Whether you are working as a cook in a small café, a baker in a local bakery, or a corporate executive in one of the Fortune 500 companies, you are still working for someone else. Most folks would agree there are fringe and benefits for the employee who works for another. If you work for a large enough company you will receive certain benefits, such as health insurance and possible retirement benefits. Large companies also offer other perks such as a matching gifts program if you are inclined to donate to a favorite charity. Many such programs will match your donation up to a specified limit. This becomes a fantastic way to improve and increase your giving! Many larger companies also have active unions which help maintain living wages, sick leave and other benefits. If your job is one of management, it will normally carry more responsibility and quite often a great deal more stress than non-managerial positions. Give and take has always been the rule. Or, better said, take and give. If you take on more responsibility you will be asking the employer to give you more financial benefits. Each person must determine for himself or herself the amount of stress they are willing to undergo in order to advance. It is not unusual for a school principal to revert back to the job of teaching in order to relieve stress. No job is worth dying for!

One of the trade-offs of working for a small company or an individual is the close personal relationship that can often be fostered. Having an employer who knows you and your children by name and may even invite you for Christmas dinner is a huge advantage in so many ways! Working for a small operation may give a sense of ownership to the employees. Often times there is the sense that we all succeed or we all fail together. Many companies even offer a profit-sharing plan when times are good. Job security is extremely important whether working for large or small employers. Doing a good job and working your hardest does not necessarily insulate you from job layoffs and downsizing when things are tough. There is no such thing as job security unless you own the company! Even if you're the owner, you still might not have a job someday.

Another consideration is the manners in which you will be paid. The overwhelming majority of the workforce will receive an hourly wage. Usually these wages are flexible and negotiable. The generally accepted rule is that the more valuable you become to your employer the more lucrative will be your reward. A high hourly wage does not necessarily guarantee a livable income. $20 an hour sounds like a good deal, unless you only are offered 25 hours a week. Then your choice becomes either find a different job or look for a second job that will fit the schedule of your first job. This is not usually an easy thing to do. I would much rather work for slightly less per hour and have a job which guaranteed at least a 40 hour week, with the possibility of overtime. It always pays to look at the big picture looking for a job. Persons involved in service jobs often have the added benefit of receiving tips. Restaurant waitresses and waiters depend heavily on their tips to earn a wage. Those who are skilled make out very well! If you are offered a salary there may be hidden expectations that are included in the job offer. You may be expected to work extra hours without extra pay. You may be expected to assume progressively greater responsibilities without any meaningful increases in your salary. It's always important to get the contract in writing and signed by whoever is doing the hiring. A written contract is like an insurance policy. It can be used to forestall disagreements and misunderstandings on both sides. Your job might well depend on this.

Many sales positions and delivery route salespersons are paid with a combination of a minimum salary plus commission on the sales they perform. Again it is important to have these figures clearly stated in writing before a job contract is signed. Salespersons should be aware of the potential for original sales figures as well as recurring sales. Which figures are being considered can make a huge difference in the amount of commission paid.

HAVE OTHER PEOPLE WORK FOR YOU

There is a certain amount of responsibility and also a great deal of freedom when you have other people working for you. The owner of a company has a responsibility to do everything possible to protect job security of his or her employees. This means doing your research and job performance in such a manner as to ensure that the company will remain viable and profitable. This may involve good advertisement and excellent job performance. Your public must know you can be trusted to offer an excellent product at a fair price every time. Your employees need to understand that having an impeccable reputation in the business community where you operate is the best guarantee of future business and continuing profits. This is also one incentive you can give your employees that they will continue to have an excellent working opportunity. If an employee understands that the boss really cares, he or she will be more motivated to excel in their performance. When this becomes a team effort, everyone wins!

HAVE A BUSINESS THAT GENERATES MONEY

There are a few businesses that by their very nature generate money all by themselves. Well, perhaps not all by themselves, but almost. An example of such a business might be owning a group of vending machines that sold individual cans of soft drinks. Or a group of vending machines that offer a chance to win a stuffed animal if the person depositing their coins has the skill to capture the stuffed animal with a set of claws in a given time. These types of business require minimum attention. The owner restarts the machine and collects the money. On occasion, maintenance needs to be performed. Still another type of business that generates its own income with little input from the owner is a coin operated laundromat. Not only is this low maintenance, but it is also virtually recession proof. Sooner or later everyone needs to do their laundry. Good customer relations along with proper maintenance on the machines and cleanliness of the establishment are important to ensure success.

HAVE YOUR MONEY WORKING FOR YOU

If your Great Uncle Henry has left you a sizable inheritance you may wish to invest these funds and literally live off the interest. Unfortunately, most of us do not have a rich Uncle Henry! However, this should not be a deterrent for having our money work for us. In the next few chapters we will discuss several different ways to begin having your money work for you. You do not need to be wealthy, merely determined and consistent.

BECOMING AN ENTREPRENEUR

If you feel that you have an entrepreneurial spirit, you may try your hand at starting a new business. Be aware that a very high percentage of new businesses fail within the first five years. If you plan to do this, it is imperative that you do your homework. Make certain you understand the nuances of the business you are planning to enter. Have a clear understanding of the competition. Have a business plan that is conservative in its estimate of future success. It is highly recommended that you submit your business plan to a person you trust who is intimately knowledgeable about that particular business. Preferably someone who has already succeeded in a similar business. There are very few businesses that can be started from scratch with no initial investment. You will have to secure start-up funds as well as sufficient funds to cover at least one year's expenses. If you feel comfortable with all of those prerequisites and the potential for failure, then go for it! Once your new business has a profitable track record, you have the possibility of selling this business for a profit. If you are gifted in this area, there is no limit to the number of times you can start a new business, build it up, and sell it. One man I know has made a living of buying older homes, restoring them and selling them for a great deal of money. One of the main secrets is to know what you're doing and do it well. If this concept excites you there are endless possibilities for you to explore.

If all else fails, borrow from your In-Laws! Or go live with your In-Laws!

CHAPTER 13 JOURNAL

WAYS TO GENERATE MONEY

What new ideas has this chapter generated?

Are you open to explore any of these?

If so, which ones make sense to you?

What is your plan of action?

SECTION FIVE

Managing Money

CHAPTER 14

A SAVINGS PLAN

Every individual and every family should have some form of a savings plan. It may seem to you that this is impossible with your present cash flow. This author believes it to be absolutely essential for every family to learn the value of a regular plan to start saving some money. There is no better time to start this process than right now. Much of the value is not monetary as much as it involves forming a state of mind. The habit of saving should be as real as the habit of brushing your teeth. It should be as much a part of you as waking up every morning. It should be as important to you as combing your hair, or shaving, or putting on makeup. When a certain action becomes a habit, it no longer requires that we give it serious thought. We simply do it. Regular, consistent saving needs to become habit-forming. It matters little how much is being saved at a time. If a child can be taught to save 10 cents a week, in 10 weeks they will have saved one dollar. If an adult starts saving with only one **dollar** a week, in 10 weeks they will have $10. Regular saving continues to add up as long as the process continues. The person doing the saving will have made it a habit and no longer thinks about how much is being set aside. When the statement comes at the end of a certain period, they will be delighted to watch their savings grow. A savings plan is a good thing because it also helps to build positive self-esteem. People with money in the bank tend to feel good about themselves! This in itself should be reward enough. Most adults are really nothing more than grown-up children. We can delight in the smallest things just like a child. By far the greatest benefit of saving is to grow an emergency fund the family can draw upon if finances become strained or suddenly interrupted. A recommended goal is that a family have a savings nest-egg equal to three months expenses for the family. Over time this can be accomplished and will act as an insurance policy during hard times.

How can I possibly do it, you may ask? One person I know shared that he had no extra money to start a savings account until he developed his own personal plan. This man disliked doing subtraction. So every time he wrote a check he entered the <u>next highest</u> whole dollar amount in his check register. This simple procedure increased his available cash by an average of $.50 for each check written. At the end of the month, if he wrote 20 checks, he would have amassed an extra $10 in his check register. Quite an easy fool-proof, system to start saving! This could also solve his subtraction problem. The young teenager who wanted to learn how to save came up with another plan. This young man placed a large glass jar in his bedroom. Every night when he came home he emptied his pockets of all his change and put it into his jar. Within a few months he had amassed a small fortune of $23.17 entirely from pocket change. Another method which is commonly used is to claim one less dependent on the income tax form filled out for the IRS. This will ensure that the IRS takes more money out of every paycheck than is necessary to cover your yearly taxes. When the "tax man" comes to your house he will be offering you a nice fat rebate! This is a painless and effective way to begin your savings program. When you receive your tax rebate, be certain to put it into a savings account of some kind before you are tempted to spend it!

Once there were two brothers, James and Jonathan Jones. James was the older brother even though they were twins. These brothers were opposites in every area of their lives. They were as different as two men could be. At the age of 10 Jonathan had a newspaper route and began saving $37 every month. James enjoyed playing video games with his friends. James would borrow games from his friends rather than try to purchase his own. 20 years later both men reached their 30th birthday on the same day! Imagine that! On the same day! On their 30th birthday the twins compared notes regarding their financial worth. James admitted that he had maxed out his visa card and his credit score had tanked. His brother Jonathan shared that he had purchased over 400 shares of Visa Incorporated over the years. One twin owed visa money he had borrowed. The other twin owned part of Visa, Inc. You figure out what happened during those 20 years! This just proves the point, where there is a will there is a way! If you have the will to start you also can think of a way to make it happen. So start thinking outside of your box! Everybody needs to have a regular savings plan.

ASSOCIATED PRESS ARTICLE

I came across the following article dated May 20, 2016 by Ken Sweet and Emily Swanson of the Associated Press. I feel compelled to share a small part of it with you.

"NEW YORK"

"Two-thirds of Americans would have difficulty coming up with the money to cover a $1000 emergency, according to an exclusive poll released Thursday, a signal that despite years of recovery from the great recession, Americans' financial conditions remain as precarious as ever. These financial difficulties span all income levels, according to the poll conducted by the Associated Press – NORC Center for Public affairs research. 75% of people in households making less than $50,000 a year would have difficulty coming up with $1,000 to cover an unexpected bill. But when income rose to between $50,000 and $100,000, the difficulty decreased only modestly to 67%. Even from the country's wealthiest 20% – households making more than $100,000 a year – 38% say they would have at least some difficulty coming up with $1,000".

I hope this information is as disturbing to you as it was to me. Hopefully, this will be one more motivation for every family to determine to start or to increase your savings accounts.

CHAPTER 14 JOURNAL

A SAVINGS PLAN

What type of savings plan do you now have?

Is it a systematic plan with regular increases?

Are your savings 'untouchable' except in emergencies?

What do you envision as the purpose for your savings?

Are you satisfied with your savings plan?

What changes do you need to make?

Are you and your spouse in agreement regarding savings?

Are compromises something you have considered?

Do you have at least $1000 saved up for emergencies?

How much $ do you have for an emergency if it happened today?

CHAPTER 15

A RETIREMENT PLAN

The only person that does not need a retirement plan is someone who expects the world to come to an end before they grow old! This person still needs a retirement plan just in case they have made a mistake. How sad to see someone who is well beyond retirement age still having to do hard labor in order to survive. There may be several reasons for this but let's hope failure to plan is not one of them. A gentleman once told me with a smile on his face that his retirement plan was to be a friendly greeter at a large department store, making certain everyone had a shopping cart to do their shopping. Thankfully he was only joking.

EMPLOYER-SPONSORED PLANS

Some of the lucky ones have a guaranteed retirement plan through their employment. These are often a combination of benefits provided by the employer or an employee trade union. Some plans offer the opportunity for the employee to contribute to his or her plan while protecting such contributions from federal taxes. If applicable, check with your employer.

<u>SOCIAL SECURITY PLANS</u>

In the United States of America there is the Social Security Administration program set up to help senior citizens financially. Many people realize that a much more detailed plan needs to be implemented to ensure financial independence during their retirement years. The Social Security Funds in the USA have been seriously depleted by successive congressional borrowing from these funds and repaying them with a worthless series of IOU notes. One of the ways Congress has devised to help deal with this shortfall is to extend the minimum eligibility age about six months for every year prior to retirement. The federal government is quick to point out that the Social Security program was never intended to finance a person's entire retirement needs. Will the Social Security be in existence for another 30 years? Nobody knows! A wise person never depends upon a source of income which is unknown.

<u>INDIVIDUAL RETIREMENT PLANS</u>

During recent years in the USA, the Federal Government has passed laws which enable individual workers to have more control over their retirement funds. Workers have the ability to set up a personal IRA, referred to as an individual retirement account, which is tax-sheltered until the owner begins to withdraw funds after retirement. Only then does the federal income tax come into play. Usually this is when the taxpayer is making less income and presumably falls into a lower tax bracket. There is another option available to individuals called the Roth IRA which taxes funds when they are initially invested but allows these funds to grow tax-free for the life of the investment. Some folks choose this as a more painless means of being taxed for their retirement funds. Rest assured that sooner or later the taxman will come knocking!

INVESTMENTS

If the family has been successful in accumulating investments these can be extremely helpful when it comes to financing retirement. Dividend income as well as funds generated by capital gains can do much to enhance one's style of life during retirement years.

INSURANCE

Whole life insurance policies accrue capital gains much like some stocks. These can be withdrawn without penalty during retirement years and used for whatever purpose the policy owner desires. Naturally if you have died before you retire this is no longer an option! It really does hold true that you cannot take it with you. Therefore, the insurance part of life insurance will benefit whoever you name as your beneficiaries. Therefore, whoever you name as beneficiaries will be the persons who benefit from your thoughtful planning. Some might claim that it pays to be nice to grandpa!

Term life insurance policies are just what the term "term" suggests. This type of insurance is normally less expensive than whole life. It offers reasonably priced coverage on a month to month basis as long as the policy premium is paid. A term policy will not accrue any cash value over time. This often is the insurance of choice for families needing coverage for only a specified period of time.

CHAPTER 15 JOURNAL

A RETIREMENT PLAN

Do you have a well-thought-out retirement plan?

Have you covered all the bases?

What changes or additions are needed?

When do you plan to update your plan?

CHAPTER 16

A CREDIT PLAN

Every person in the USA needs to know their credit score. There are three credit rating companies in the USA, each of which gives its own version of your credit worthiness. Each of these companies use their own complex system in order to arrive at your magic number. This can be a number from a low of 600 to a perfect score of 850. Your individual credit score is used by many different organizations. If you want to buy a couch or an automobile your credit score will be the very first factor which will determine how much credit you will be offered, as well as the percentage of interest, you will be charged. A credit check is often used to approve a renter before a rental agreement is signed. Without a good credit score it is very difficult to obtain a Real Estate Loan needed to buy a home or a Small Business Loan necessary to launch any type of business. Indeed, your credit score is king! So, God save the King!

What information is used to determine this magic number? The credit rating company will do what is called a credit check where they access all of your public financial records. This includes credit card transactions and balances as well as payment history on larger items such as an automobile which is financed and all real estate loans. Then they will crunch the numbers to determine if your debt load is reasonable when compared to your income. If they discover any history of late payments or missed payments your credit score will be lowered accordingly. Many families strive for a number in the mid-to high seven-hundreds. Anyone holding a score of 750 or more is highly favored among lending institutions.

This author has a general rule concerning credit. Each family should own no more than two major credit cards. One of these may be used for regular purchases of any kind just as long as they are paid in full every month. This is an excellent way to earn bonus credits, or airline miles, if you choose. If you choose to do this, *it is imperative* that the balance be paid in full every month! Paying your credit card in full each month will do a great deal to raise your credit score. Make certain you do not fall into the credit card trap whereby you start paying less than the total every month. If you start to carry a running balance on your credit card two things are bound to happen. You will be charged a whopping amount of monthly interest, and you will imperil your credit score rating! Please do not get caught up in this deadly trap!

Another golden rule: never give a credit card to a child under 18! Scientists claim that the brain of a child does not fully develop until at least age 25. With this in mind, who would possibly want to give a credit card to a teenager? Do so at your own peril. Quite often they will spend you into bankruptcy, and never realize what they've done. Don't even allow a teenager to borrow your credit card. They have no idea the damage they can do!

The second credit card should be considered your backup card and should be reserved for emergencies, large item purchases that are necessities, and expenses such as airline tickets. Credit cards used in any other way can become an insidious financial anchor around the neck of the cardholder. Golden rule of finance, if you cannot afford to pay for it, do not purchase it! The only exception, in my opinion, is for purchases that will increase in value over time, such as your house or other real estate. Personal household debt in the United States has mushroomed and become totally unmanageable for many households! Often the only solution is to declare personal bankruptcy. This will negatively impact a person's credit worthiness for a minimum of 7 years. Credit is a wonderful tool, but only if used wisely! If we wish to see an example of spending beyond the ability to pay, we need merely to look at the federal government as the most terrible example. Our Congress has spent this country into a debt that may never be able to be repaid. Our elected leaders have burdened our children and grandchildren with a tremendous national debt. Every family needs to look at the spending example of the US government and vow never to do the same!

If you wish to find out your credit score, simply go online and visit USA credit reports. The site is mobile friendly and you will find out how to get your credit report, make corrections, and more. Every person is entitled to a free credit report yearly from each of the three main credit reporting agencies. These include Equifax, LifeLock, and Experien. Again this is a simple matter of going online and searching for each of these companies. You will be asked to fill out a short information form and within minutes you will have your FREE complete credit report in your hands. Not only will this give you your credit score, but also a detailed analysis of how you can improve your score by taking certain actions. You may need to close out certain credit accounts. You may need to lower your credit balance on all your accounts. You may need to pay attention and commit to paying your bills on time. Whatever action is needed, you can improve your credit score with a minimum of effort on your part. I highly recommend you do this as soon as possible. You, and you alone, will benefit from an improved credit score. Rest assured your credit score will follow you all the days of your life. It has the power to become your best friend or your worst enemy imaginable. Much like death and taxes, you cannot escape your credit score! So embrace it!

CHAPTER 16 JOURNAL

A CREDIT PLAN

It is imperative for every family to have their credit under control!

How do you rate your family credit score? from 0% to 100%? With 100% being excellent.

Now, what is your official credit score?

Do you have long-term credit card charges or balances?

List these:

Are you able to explain the danger of credit card debt?

If so, what is your plan to pay off your credit card balances?

If necessary, are you willing to ask for professional help?

Where would you begin to look?

If you are not willing to get help, why not? Try to be honest!

Does personal pride come into play here?

Will you feel embarrassed if you need to ask for help?

Are you willing to swallow your pride and get the help you need?

CHAPTER 17

AN INVESTMENT PLAN

Holy cow!! We can just barely make ends meet now and you want us to think about investing? This seems to be the normal reaction from most families in the middle income brackets. Let me assure you that investing is very similar to saving. I invite you to turn back to chapter 14, the chapter on savings. Read that chapter again, reflectively. Does the rationale of saving in a disciplined, consistent, manner makes sense to you? If you agree with that rationale, the discipline of regular investing is very similar. Many folks never investigate the concept of investing. The average person feels one must be wealthy in order to become an investor. This just is not true! In fact, just the opposite is true! There are many ways that the average wage earner can participate in the stock market. Does this surprise you? Let's look at a few of these.

MUTUAL FUNDS

The simplest method to begin investing is to consider purchasing mutual funds. There are as many different kinds of mutual funds as there are dandelions in your front lawn. Attempting a detailed analysis is beyond the scope of this book. However, a few basic facts may be helpful. You do not need a broker to purchase mutual funds. Most mutual funds are considered to be "open ended" meaning simply that they are open to anyone who wishes to purchase them. The author suggests you look for "no-load funds" which simply means there is no charge for opening your account or for purchasing additional shares whenever you wish. This being said, perhaps the safest type of mutual fund in the US is what is referred to as an "Index Fund". Simply put, this type of a fund will purchase a variety of socks in many companies attempting to correlate with one of the main stock indexes such as the industrial 500. This index is a compilation of 500 of the more widely known and successful businesses in the USA. There are several reputable companies which offer this type of mutual fund. Among them are the Vanguard family of funds, American family of funds and several others. This is about as safe an investment as is possible for the beginning investor. Once you have opened an account most companies will allow you to make small investments on a regular basis. When these investments are incorporated into your budget they become as painless as buying a tank of gasoline for your car. You will scarcely miss your regular deposits into the funds and they will grow over time. It is generally suggested that the novice investor not try to "time-the-market", but instead leave their funds alone while allowing them to grow. Simply having an invested stake in the future of your family should bring a happy grin to your face and a certain lightness to your steps. If you have children who are young, this may even help to pay college tuition or at the very least to finance a wedding.

TEACHING CHILDREN

Many years ago, after being discharged from the Navy, this author landed a job teaching mathematics to eighth graders in California. One class was made up of exceptionally gifted students who were looking for new challenges. This teacher decided to help these children become vested in the US stock market. Each student was issued $10,000 in 'make-believe' money. Several days were spent teaching the students how to read the daily stock market reports. Next they were taught how to do research on individual companies. The students were allowed to purchase make-believe stock in their company of choice. At the end of each week students were given the opportunity to make an oral report on the progress of the company or companies they had invested in. This teacher kept a graph of the different companies gains or losses over the period of one month. The students learned many important lessons about investing during that month. Perhaps this is one class that might be offered on a large scale to many advanced students throughout the nation. It's fair to say that most of these kids no longer feared investing when they became adults. In fact, many quite probably looked forward to the exercise and the potential profits.

This author found ways to make learning fun for the average students as well. These students were also issued a certain amount of play money representing the cost of food for an average family for one week. The students were taught how to evaluate true bargains from advertising hype. They were taught how to figure such things as cost per ounce and comparative values for large and small packaging of the same product. Many times they were amazed that the large economy size of a product was actually more expensive than a smaller size. This was especially true when the smaller sizes were on sale. The students were taught selective value shopping. An imaginary grocery store was set up and shopping trips were planned each week. The same concept could be enhanced with a family trip to an actual store. They had fun while learning many basic values that could be applied to their shopping habits for the rest of their lives. And who said mathematics could not be fun?

This author believes that parents have a wonderful opportunity to become the teachers of their children in many true-to-life situations. If you have teenage children that are struggling with mathematics why not help them learn such real-life skills while also mastering basic mathematics. This can also branch out into learning percentages and conversions like ounces to pounds and metric measurements as well. Parents can have a lot of fun interacting with their children and teaching them at the same time. Lessons in saving and percentages along with interest rates lend themselves well to this type activity. Using a little ingenuity and lots of energy parents can help kids realize learning can be fun! If you, the parent, are not willing to invest in your child's future, who else will? I urge you to get involved in your child's future while they are still young enough to allow it to happen. There is a common perception among youth that parents have less and less wisdom as the years go by. So get smart, and get involved with your kids while they will still let you.

Happy investing!

CHAPTER 17 JOURNAL

AN INVESTMENT PLAN

Do you have an investment plan?

Refresh your memory by writing it down!

Are your investments in line with your risk-comfort zone?

Is your spouse involved? If not, why not?

What is your plan and timeline to involve your spouse?

CHAPTER 18
AN INSURANCE PLAN

Almost every family needs to have an insurance plan. The obvious exception might be an elderly couple whose children are raised and who have a nice great big fat financial bank account. Personally I don't know many such people. Like any investment, the sooner a policy is purchased the more protection one can buy for the least amount of money. I mean golly gee, this just makes so much sense! As an example, grandparents are offered policies on their grandchildren for just a few dollars a year for the first 20 years or more. The beauty of such a policy is that it becomes a whole life policy at a certain age and can then continue throughout the life of the child with a guarantee of continued acceptance. It is sad that many people do not think of insurance until they have some medical condition, quite often making themselves no longer insurable, or at the very least raising the rates to a point that insurance is no longer a viable financial consideration.

Most insurance companies offer two basic types of life insurance. Whole Life is a policy that acts in many ways like any other investment. There is the face value which is the amount the company will pay your next of kin upon your death. There is also the potential for this face value to increase over time depending on the experience of the insurance company. Another advantage of a whole life policy is that it not only grows in value but after time it accumulates a certain amount of loan value. This allows the owner to withdraw certain funds while maintaining the complete insurance coverage. Whole life policies have an added value because they can be transferred from the original owner to the owner's estate, thereby benefiting generations to come. It is important when writing a will to specifically include any life insurance policy that you wish to include as part of your estate. Be certain to include the certificate number and the issuing company as well as the physical location of the insurance papers. It is important to specify who is the owner of the policy as well as who is the beneficiary. It is also important to record any changes that the owner of the policy chooses to make. If a person already has a will and wishes to change it, a simple addition can easily be made. If you have any complex situations it is always wise to seek the wisdom of an attorney. Some of the inexpensive online programs may work well enough for a simple document but many are limited. Remember this is your last will and testimony so it pays to get right the first time.

Term life policies offer basic insurance coverage with none of the added benefits. A Term life policy will expire when it ceases to be funded. Term life policies are exceptionally valuable when the insurance need is for a predictable period of time. When funds are limited, a Term life policy is a wise choice. Life insurance is important, so don't leave this earth without it.

CHAPTER 18 JOURNAL

AN INSURANCE PLAN

Make a list of all your policies, including all pertinent information

Go over this with your spouse, making changes as needed.

Put this information in a safe place where everyone knows its location

SECTION SIX

Understanding Principles

CHAPTER 19
RISK ASSESMENT

Risk assessment is a term used in financial circles to determine your degree of tolerance for unknown variables. This is a series of tests you can give to yourself only if you understand the importance of how you make decisions. Do you have an analytical character where you carefully weigh and evaluate every decision? Or are you more emotional and tend to listen to your gut reaction. What kind of a poker player would you be? Would you wildly bet on a less than average looking hand? Or are you so conservative that it would take a hand full of three kings and four aces before you would bet the farm? Many investors make a fundamental error by becoming emotionally attached to their investments. It might be some stock that Grandpa handed down which means a great deal to you. Are you wise enough to sell that stock when all indicators predict this company will 'tank' in the next few weeks? Or would you dutifully hang onto the stock certificate and frame it as a picture on the wall even though it has become monetarily worthless? This is a rudimentary look at the concept of risk assessment.

If you still don't understand what I'm talking about, please don't invest even one nickel of your wealth! Every investor needs to carefully evaluate his or her comfort zone including a basic understanding of risk tolerance. Your personality determines to a great extent the amount of risk you should take in your investments. New investors should beware of all get-rich-quick schemes! Ask yourself the question: "If this is such a wonderful opportunity, why doesn't everyone jump in immediately?" It may be wise to stick with a philosophy on investing only in companies you understand. With household names that are familiar. Companies that make products or offer services you understand and can endorse.

Moral responsibility needs to be at least of equal importance as financial considerations when choosing investments. As an example, do you feel that a Christian should invest in a company making products known to cause cancer, such as cigarettes? Or a company manufacturing alcoholic beverage? Or even a fast-food company with products known to cause heart failure and obesity? How important is it to you for Christ to be the central focal point of <u>all</u> your financial decisions?

You may be so conservative that you will never risk your money in any other place than in a Federal Government Insured savings account. You may need this assurance to sleep at night. There is absolutely nothing wrong with this.

It merely suggests that you have a very low tolerance for risk. While you will never grow rich with this approach, you may sleep better at night than most. Just one word of caution, the word is "inflation". In almost every country in the civilized world, the value of currency will never remain unchanged. As of the writing of this book, the inflation rate in the USA is extremely low. Low inflation rates normally translate into low interest rates as well. Most savings accounts and certificates of deposit currently earn less than 1% per year. With inflation predicted to be 3 ½ or 4% per year it does not take a mathematical genius to figure out that your currency left in a savings account, or under your mattress, will continue to shrink in purchasing power unless you take some steps to correct this. Inflation is one of the main reasons that a portion of your funds needs to be generating some form of interest just to stay even. Chapter 20 will investigate different methods of accomplishing this task.

CHAPTER 19 JOURNAL

RISK ASSESSMENT

Are you a risk taker?Yes___No___Not sure____

How aggressive do you feel you should be with your investments?

Are you tempted to borrow money in order to invest?

How does your marriage partner compare to you as a risk taker?

Take time to explain your differences so that you understand them.

Talk about these with your spouse before making financial decisions.

CHAPTER 20

DIVIDENDS AND CAPITAL GAINS

You may be the type of person who is extremely conservative in nature. You may not be able to sleep at night unless your savings are in a safe place, such as a savings account or a certificate of deposit fully insured by the federal government. If you are this person this is great. You may never become rich but you probably will not stay awake nights worrying about the safety of your money. You may not understand or even care about inflation. If this is you, I suggest you sail on past this chapter and go to something more to your liking.

For the rest of you let's have some fun. Back in chapter 17 the author suggested that every family and every individual should have some type of an investment plan. Chapter 17 went on to examine an extremely safe and conservative possibility. The author suggested that anyone with a very small amount of money can begin investing through mutual funds. If this is your desire, I respectfully suggest you proceed with your plan.

If you like the idea of a more hands-on approach to investing, may I invite you to keep on reading. What does the word drip mean to you? This word has a specific meaning in the world of finance. It stands for dividend reinvestment program. Many of the larger, more established companies in the USA offer an opportunity for individual investors to become shareholders in their company. Here's how it works. Most of these companies require that a person purchase one single share in the company. This is usually accomplished through a brokerage house that has this type of relationship with the company. For an example, let's say you want to start a DRIP purchase program with company XYZ. You go on the Internet and Google up "XYZ stocks". When you open the company web page you will be directed how to sign up for their drip program. After you have purchased a single share, which typically will cost less than $100, you then have the opportunity to sign up for automatic monthly purchases which will be deducted from your checking account. These companies value new investors, and because of this they make it extremely easy for you to progressively purchase their shares. If the company pays dividends on their stocks, they usually give you the opportunity to reinvest the periodic dividends paid to you. These dividends then purchase additional shares in the company. If you are a person who enjoys owning stock in one or more individual companies, then perhaps this program is 'tailor-made' for your personality. This author has purchased stocks in this manner for many years. He finds it educational and rather exciting to watch his personal wealth accumulate.

What is the difference between interest, dividends, and capital gains? All three are designed to make money and to meet or exceed inflation. Most people understand that interest is paid on money deposited into some form of interest-bearing account. Does this account pay simple interest or is the interest compounded? If it is compounded how often does this take place? Compounded interest works very much the same as dividend reinvestment's. Whatever dividends are earned, they are periodically added to the principal balance, thereby providing a larger principle balance, which will in turn generate interest. In other words, your interest you have earned is earning additional interest over time.

Dividends are a form of interest paid by companies to their stockholders based on the number of shares that are owned. Dividends are calculated as a percentage of the current share price of an individual share in the company at the time the dividend is paid. Many companies pay dividends several times a year, either periodically or on a fixed schedule. If a company is paying 5% dividend on a quarterly basis and the share price continues to increase, the dollar amount of the dividend will also increase proportionately. When these dividends are re-invested in additional stock purchases, the results can multiply quite rapidly. This is also known as compounding.

Capital gains are represented when the purchase or selling price of a company's stock increases. Capital gains are reported in the portfolio of each individual stockholder normally on a quarterly basis. Assuming your stock XYZ was purchased at a share price of $10 and the company value increased to a share price of $17. You would have a net gain of seven dollars per share. This can happen over a period of time or as quickly as a few hours. That's what makes it so exciting!

Let me offer some cautions. Never invest in a company you do not thoroughly investigate and feel confident about. The beginning investor should probably not invest in a company that does not produce a product or service. If you like the way a certain hamburger company does business, you may wish to purchase some of their shares as well as their hamburgers. Just make certain this is not a fly-by-night hamburger company. You might also check the hamburgers for flies! The secret to wise investing is to investigate each company before you purchase. Another caution might be to never invest more money in any one company than you could comfortably afford to lose. If you have invested wisely, there is the strong probability that any losses you may suffer will be small. Bear in mind "that any losses" never become actual dollar losses unless you choose to sell the stock when the price is low. Many small investors and some larger ones make all the wrong moves at the wrong time. If the stock's price begins to drop, this in itself is not a reason to sell. In fact, this may be the perfect opportunity to buy more stock while the price is cheaper! Always remember there has never been a person in the history of the stock market who was able to successfully predict the timing of the rise and fall of the market. So don't even try

If you want nothing to do with a drip program, you will need a stockbroker to facilitate your purchase of stock of any individual, publicly traded company. Fortunately, these are readily available. There are several brokerages that will sign you up and charge you a small amount for each transaction. Usually this is between five and nine dollars per transaction. Yes, my friend, in today's world anyone can own stock. Especially you! It's sort of like learning to swim. The first step is to enter the water. The next step is to find a qualified teacher who will help you learn to swim. It is never wise to jump into deep water before you learn to swim. The same can be said of entering the stock market.

CHAPTER 20 JOURNAL

DIVIDENDS AND CAPITAL GAINS

Are you serious about starting to invest?

How serious? Are you willing to spend a little time and resources to educate yourself?

Will you subscribe to one or more finance magazines?

Will you visit the public library and read newspapers like the Wall Street Journal?

CHAPTER 21
SHORT TERM – LONG TERM

In any financial transaction one of the questions that needs to be asked, "What is the time-frame of this transaction?" As a general rule, the longer the time of a contract, the more expensive that contract becomes. If you are going to purchase a house, most mortgage companies will give you a much better percentage rate for a 20 - year loan versus a 30 - year loan. Conversely, if you invest your money for a long period of time it will normally earn a greater return than the same amount of money invested for a short period. When you have resources that won't be needed in the foreseeable future, this gives you a great deal more leverage than short-term investing would allow. This is the 'long and the short' of finance!

Another way of earning money is to invest in bonds. The federal government offers to sell US savings bonds to individuals in denominations as small as $50 and as large as several thousand dollars. This is an excellent way for the small investor to get started. Your money is safe and the interest rate consistently beats what the banks are offering! Many banks offer this service to their customers whereby the bank handles the transaction for you to purchase these bonds. Keep in mind that US savings bonds are long-term investments.

There are also several mutual funds that invest only in bonds. These funds invest mostly in corporate bonds. All mutual funds dealing with bonds have a specific safety rating system in place that is quite standard throughout the industry. Bonds traditionally offer more safety than stocks. With greater safety comes a smaller financial reward. The short and the long of bond investing follows the same principle. Most long-term bonds pay higher interest than short-term bonds, primarily due to the different exposure times. As a general rule, when stock prices go up the price of corporate bonds goes down. The reverse is true, when the price of stocks goes down the price of corporate bonds will generally rise. Let me stress once again, do your homework! Educate yourself by doing your research online or at the local library. Caution, well-meaning friends are not necessarily your best source of good and reliable information. If you are planning to purchase bond mutual funds, again make certain you deal only with well-known firms with excellent ratings. There are two parts to the basic formula for evaluating interest rates.

PAYING INTEREST

When purchasing anything on credit you will be asked to sign a purchase contract. The shorter your repayment time, the less amount of interest you will pay. If you choose to stretch out the timeframe, your payments may be smaller but your interest will be considerably greater.

Always make the contract reflect the largest amount you can reasonably pay on a monthly basis. This will automatically reduce the total amount of interest you will pay over the long term.

EARNING INTEREST

When earning interest just the opposite is true. An example might be that you sell an automobile and you agree to "carry the note" meaning that you will accept a down payment on your sale and accept regular payments including a pre-determined interest rate. The longer the contract, the more money you will make in interest, however the monthly payments will be smaller. If you choose to carry the note for any item which you sell, make sure to get a written contract. Only do this for someone you know and trust will make their payments on time. You should adjust your interest rates upwards if they request a longer period of repayment. It is also wise to include a late payment fee clause in the contract.

CHAPTER 21 JOURNAL

SHORT TERM – LONG TERM

How do you determine if you need to borrow money?

If you borrow money, which format will you choose?

Long-term debt with greater interest rate?

Short-term loan with lower interest rate?

CHAPTER 22

MIRACLE OF COMPOUNDING

The miracle of compounding has been touched upon in previous chapters. Quite simply it is the principle of multiplication as compared to addition. Adding 3+3+3+3 = 12. Multiplication is a vastly different concept, 3×3×3×3 = 81. Any third grade student knows the difference between 12 pennies and 81 pennies. Compounding is not quite as simple as this, but almost. Example number one: Mr. Jones deposits $10,000 in his savings account which pays 5% simple interest every year for a period of 10 years. This means Mr. Jones will earn 5% of $10,000, or $500 every year for 10 years. At the end of 10 years he will have collected $5,000 in interest. Mr. Simpson also deposits $10,000 in his bank's savings account at the same time. Only Mr. Simpson is offered 5% compound interest, compounded twice a year. Let's get out our calculators and figure the difference. At the end of six months Mr. Simpson receives $250 interest making his balance $10,250. At the end of the first year Mr. Simpson's interest payment is $256.25 leaving him the balance of $10,506.25. Six months later Mr. Simpson receives an interest payment of $262.66 giving him a total of $10,768.90. At the end of year two Mr. Simpson receives an interest payment of $269.22 giving him a total of $11,038.12. By the end of year 10, Mr. Simpson will have received a staggering $8,052in interest, compared to Mr. Jones who would have received a mere $5,000. Compounding the interest payments would have added over $3,000 during the same ten-year period. Compound interest makes a significant difference. It takes very little imagination to project how important this will become for a real estate loan of $250,000 over a period of 30 years! When it is time to negotiate any contract, it pays to carefully read the fine print.

As a general rule, most real estate transactions charge simple interest. This is also true of most large purchases such as automobiles. The general rule is you want to pay simple interest when you are being charged by someone else and you would like to earn compound interest when your money is invested with someone else. Hopefully this makes sense.

CHAPTER 22 JOURNAL

MIRACLE OF COMPOUNDING

Write down your understanding of the difference between earning simple interest and earning compound interest.

Now, on the flip side, write down the reasons you would not wish to pay compounded interest when you purchase a home or an automobile. Be very specific!

CHAPTER 23

HOUSING DECISIONS

Many factors go into the decisions a family makes when deciding how they are going to live. If a family member has an adequate credit score, there are many more choices available. When a credit score is below average, the possibility of finding good housing diminishes greatly. Under these circumstances it is probable that the only choice is to find a rental unit. In the present rental market many landlords do a credit check on perspective tenants. This author cannot stress enough the importance of maintaining a good credit score. Let's assume you are able to consider purchasing a home. This may not be the wisest choice. A major consideration will be the length of your expected tenancy. Would you be moving in just a few years or do you plan to stay for a longer time? There is a very real danger in purchasing a home for a short period of time. If forced to move, it may be difficult to quickly sell a home, especially if the market is not favorable. Under normal circumstances short tenancy suggests renting rather than buying. If the family plans to stay in the same location for an extended period of time, purchasing a home would seem to be the wiser choice. Most real estate properties will appreciate over time and may become your most valuable investment. In the early years of home purchase a large portion of each payment goes towards interest. Even so, the home owner is accruing value in the property. In the USA, interest paid on the purchase of a primary residence is considered deductible for federal income taxes.

Once more we need to look at the long and the short consequences of home investment. With every monthly payment, a little bit more of the payment is credited to principle and less to interest. After several years this becomes quite significant, as the homeowner gains more and more equity in the home. The current health of the housing market is another significant concern. How fast are houses being sold? Is the price of local housing high or are prices depressed? It is important to understand that buying a house is exactly like any other investment. This being said, purchasing a house has many other considerations such as normal costs of maintenance and upkeep, like mowing the lawn and making small repairs. Owning a house also incurs periodic large expenses such as adding a new roof every 15 or 20 years, and repainting as needed. Other major expenses to consider will be property taxes payable every year along with the cost of homeowner insurance.

Some of the advantages to owning a house include having the freedom to make whatever changes you wish without needing to gain approval from the owners. If the owner wants to put nails in the wall to hang up a picture, there are no restrictions! Home ownership gives the feeling that you are master or mistress of your own domain.

Location is the most important single factor when considering the purchase of a home. A real estate agent was asked to name the three most important factors to consider when purchasing a home. The answer given was, location, location, location! A modest home in a good location is quite often preferable to a more elaborate home in a less desirable neighborhood. These are a few of the more important factors to consider as you explore the possibility of purchasing a home. Finding a responsible, honest, realtor is extremely important during this process.

When looking to rent a home it is important to understand local laws and restrictions imposed upon tenants. Most cities have specific rules and regulations that govern both the perspective tenants and the landlord. It is important to understand the difference between a month-to-month rental agreement and a term lease agreement. Each type has its advantages and its drawbacks. It is incumbent on the prospective tenant to make this determination before starting the process of searching for a suitable place to live. The wise prospective renters will determine in advance how much they can afford each month for the rent. It's also wise to check out the neighborhood to determine the availability of good schools if you have school-age children. Many folks like to check out the availability of a church of their choosing within a reasonable distance as well. Oh my, all these decisions!

There are numerous upfront hidden costs when planning to purchase a home. Such things as testing to ensure there is no lead-containing paint on any portion of the buildings. Inspection for termite and dryrot damage. At times there is the requirement for inspection by a structural engineer to inspect the foundation and roof. Most of these are not optional since the banks or lending institution will probably require them. Almost all lending institutions will require a professional appraisal by a licensed real estate appraiser prior to generating a real estate loan. Yes, this also costs more money! Professional real estate agents will collect a minimum of 6% commission upon closing any real estate transaction. The final chunk of cash needed to purchase a home is known as the down payment which is typically 20% of the purchase price to be paid at the close of escrow. Beware of the loan that brags about the low down payment. These loans typically make up the difference by charging a higher interest rate. There will be other added expenses such as escrow fees, title search, and title insurance just to name a few. If you have never purchased a home before, these expenses may seem overwhelming. Repeat buyers know that this is just the cost of doing business when purchasing real estate. It's small wonder that so many families have no choice but to rent their home. Renters can and often do save money over time to purchase a home in lieu of renting. For many years, home ownership has become a symbol of achieving the American dream!

The decision to buy a home has financial advantages as well as certain costs. The value of the home is normally the largest single investment for the average family.

Purchased homes represent a significant proportion of the net worth of most families. When a primary residence is purchased, all interest payments are tax deductible under federal tax code. This can be very advantageous when the taxman comes knocking! There are several other financial advantages to purchasing a home as long as it remains the primary residence of the owner. If you make a profit when it comes time to sell the home this is considered a capital gain by the federal government. Normally capital gains are taxed just like income with the following exception, if the homeowner buys another home within one year all the capital gains are rolled over into the new home resulting in the tax burden of zero. Now this can become very rewarding! This tax benefit can be repeated over and over again as long as each succeeding home purchase takes place within the one-year time frame.

Enough of all this, the author feels like an instructor in a real estate class at a junior college! Far from it! This author has gained his vast wealth of knowledge mainly through the school of hard knocks. His first home cost $20,000 with $2,000 as a down payment. The realtor, who was a friend, had to loan this author $300 towards the down payment in order to close the deal! He also allowed his commission to be paid over a period of time. Those were days when a simple handshake was all that was needed. My, how times have changed. Scripture suggests that all transactions can be that simple. It states that a man's word should be his bond. Somehow, the world has strayed far from what God envisioned for mankind.

CHAPTER 23 JOURNAL

HOUSING DECISIONS

List all the housing factors you need to consider starting with the most important, and continue in descending order of importance.

Place an*before those factors that are non-negotiable.

Explain to yourself why!

SECTION SEVEN

Family Dynamics

CHAPTER 24

DETERMINING OWNERSHIP

This author has conducted many family interviews concerning finances. Oftentimes it seemed more like acting as a referee between two opposing forces! Jesus taught that lusting after money was the very root of all that is evil in this world. Money represents power. Power represents control of one person over another. Power represents control of one group over another. Money equals power and power equals money. They go together and perhaps they always have. One of the most basic questions concerns ownership. Who's money is it and whose money should it be? Who deserves it the most? A more basic question might be "what determines ownership?" These and similar concerns represent a great deal of the conflict in many families. Most marriage counselors agree that money issues represent much of the conflict. This is greater than any other single issue. Money is not the culprit here, but the control of money seems to be the culprit we're dealing with.

Who controls the money can quickly become the issue that divides and destroys a family. Often the wage earner has a strong feeling that he or she owns the money that they have worked for. On the surface this seems to be a reasonable assumption. In families when there is more than one wage earner this question becomes more complex. The real issue seems to center around the question of power rather than money. It becomes critical for a family to decide these issues in a loving and fair-minded matter if there is going to be peace and tranquility! At this point it could be helpful to re-examine chapters on budgets. One of the reasons for making a budget and sticking to it deals with the issues of control. If all the family income gets put in one pot and co-mingled, then it no longer becomes his and hers. When family income is co-mingled in such a way as to become indistinguishable as to origin it then becomes neither his nor hers, instead it becomes family property! This might be referred to as a one-pot financial solution! Never let the love of money control and conquer a beautiful love relationship. It simply makes little sense to allow the control of money to fracture the harmony of a family. Life is just too short! Families need to remember the old saying "you can't take it with you"! A much better approach would be to use it for the benefit of all. Let's use our combined resources to meet the needs and future expectations of our family unit. Now doesn't this sound wise? Wouldn't you say this fits into the definition of a Christ centered financial plan? Isn't it possible that this could lead to peace and tranquility within the family unit? Then let's give it a try!

It is usually advisable to include both husband and wife as joint owners with right of survivorship on major financial documents such as when purchasing a home, automobile, or any type of financial account. If a man and woman are willing to share their life together, certainly sharing their financial burdens and benefits are part of the deal. Christ centered finances are one tool to strengthen Christ centered families. You will learn more about this in the third book of this series entitled "Christ Centered Families" 'Your Kids Matter'.

CHAPTER 24 JOURNAL

DETERMINING OWNERSHIP

What are the major money issues in your family today?

How have these caused friction in your relationships?

Specifically, how do you plan to solve these?

When, if it at all, do you think outside help is needed?

CHAPTER 25
WRITTEN AGREEMENTS

It seems, as we get older, the thing we miss the most is our memory. By the time we realize it's missing we have no idea where to find it. We just wake up some morning to realize that things just seem a bit 'more-fuzzy' than they were before. At some point it becomes necessary to recognize this fact and adjust accordingly. One of the simplest solutions is to quit depending on memory and begin to write things down. A written record doesn't change its mind! A written document does not even lose its mind! There are times when this author does not even remember that he has a mind! What did you have for breakfast three Saturdays ago? See that, I'll bet you cannot remember. And that's only three weeks ago. What can you possibly remember that was agreed upon three years ago? "The sad answer probably is "very little". I rest my case, write it down and put it where others you trust know where to find it. Many families find it advantageous to own a small safe or to rent a safe deposit box in the local bank. However, there is no value in a safe that is empty! Written records that are important enough to put in writing are also important enough to put in one safe place. Safe storage equals safe recovery. Safe recovery depends on the location of the safe place. Under the mattress is never a safe place. Besides, too many papers would make it lumpy and uncomfortable.

As parents grow older they often promise certain memorable belongings to different children or other relatives. This can become a problem if they forget what was promised to whom. When grandma promises both Mary and Martha the same piece of precious jewelry and subsequently she forgot what she had promised, this can cause divisions in the family that she never intended. Here's a better plan, write it down. If as in the case of Mary and Martha, make sure each party has a copy of your wishes. No one has to count on remembering.

There is the story of two twin sisters who had lived together all their lives. As they grew older each sister began to lose her memory but denied this fact to the other. Finally, they each agreed to write memos to themselves in order to jog the memory. Since they were twins and both of them had similar handwriting they decided to use different colors for their notepaper. One sister used blue paper, the other green. This worked out well until neither sister could remember which color represented her own notes. To solve this confusion, they decided that one sister would write in capital letters and the other one would use nothing but lowercase letters. Sure enough both sisters forgot who was using which case. Both sisters finally decided that written notes were not such a good idea after all. They both went back to relying upon their memories which were quickly fading. So ends this silly story. The moral of the story is write it down and keep the written record in a safe place. Never leave this to memory! Such a terrible thing to lose.

It's important to have one single location for storing important documents, such as a filing cabinet, a small family safe, or a safe deposit box. This should be agreed upon by both parties and all important documents stored in one place. Make certain other family members know where to look for your written documents. Wisdom dictates we should never use the memory bank of a computer as a substitute for written records on real paper in a specific location. Keeping records in a Microsoft cloud or on a hard drive of your old computer is risky business. What if the cloud evaporates or the hard drive crashes? An even bigger possibility is that you forget your password and therefore cannot access your precious documents! How embarrassing will that be? This author has forgotten more passwords than he can remember!

CHAPTER 25 JOURNAL

WRITTEN AGREEMENTS

Which agreements do you have in writing?

Do you feel that these are sufficient?

List new agreements you plan to put in written form.

CHAPTER 26

FORMAL DOCUMENTS

WRITING YOUR WILLS

Every person should have a written will no matter what your age may be. Many folks do not consider writing a will until they reach retirement age. This is totally unwise! The question may be raised about the need for a will at a young age. One of the great facts of life is that everyone is going to die! This means you! The question is, *when* are you going to die, not if! Therefore, it is imperative that you help out those left behind by providing a written document explaining your desires when this event happens. Often the term "an untimely death" is used to describe the passing of a younger person. While this is sad, it is much more difficult when that person has died intestate. This simply means without a will. In many states in the USA, if a person dies without a written will, the next of kin has no say in the disposition of any possessions left behind. It simply becomes a matter of the State or a local court deciding what happens. One of the unspoken reasons for delaying this important job seems to be the fear that once a will is written, a person will probably die. Everyone knows this is complete foolishness. Foolish or not, this often happens. Back to the original statement, every person needs to have a written will. In most states a simple handwritten document, witnessed and signed by two adults, is sufficient to be recognized in a court of law. This is the bare minimum requirement for most families. A much better plan would be to hire an attorney who specializes in probate law. He or she will be able to ask the appropriate questions and record the document in a legally recognized format to avoid possible problems after you die.

Your attorney may be helpful in suggesting an appropriate person to act as the executor of your estate. You will should instruct the executive concerning beneficiaries and distribution of specific properties. It is hoped that all Christians will seriously consider leaving a significant portion of their estate to the local church and other Christian ministries of their choosing.

FAMILY TRUSTS

Under certain circumstances it is advisable to set up a family trust. This may be a valuable method of combining most family assets to make it easier for the executor of the estate to distribute assets either before or after an untimely death or disability. A Family Trust is a convenient way to ensure proper financing for the care of minor children. It is imperative to include signed wills as part of any family trust. Copies of insurance policies also need to be included. A special needs trust is a vehicle to enable a family to set aside certain funds for the care of a family member who is disabled. This type of trust has many tax advantages as well as certain limitations and should never be attempted without the help of an attorney. Proper attention needs to be paid as to how a trust is to be funded either at its inception or sometime in the future. Every trust must specify the name and address of the assigned trustee along with certain instructions to the trustee.

PRE-NUPITAL AGREEMENTS

In certain rare occasions, it may be deemed wise for a couple to write out a document protecting individual assets owned by one or the other before a marriage is consummated. It is the opinion of this author that prenuptial agreements have no place in a Christ Centered financial arrangement! This type of document is best left for the extremely wealthy who have developed a severe lack of trust!

CHAPTER 26 JOURNAL

FORMAL DOCUMENTS

List your formal documents.

Where are these located?

Does everyone in your family know where to find them?

What other formal documents do you feel that you need?

SECTION EIGHT

Using Money

CHAPTER 27
TO CONTROL AND TO DECEIVE

In the book of Acts, we read a sobering story about a couple in the early church who attempted to use money as a vehicle for power and control. "There was a man named Ananias who, with his wife, Sophria, sold some property. He brought part of the money to the apostles, but he claimed it was the full amount. His wife had agreed to this deception. Then Peter said, Ananias, why has Satan filled your heart? You lied to the Holy Spirit, and you kept some of the money for yourself. The property was yours to sell or not to sell, as you wish. And after selling it, the money was yours to give away. How could you do a thing like this? You weren't lying to us but to God." As soon as Ananias heard these words he fell to the floor and died. Everyone who heard about this was terrified. Then some young men wrapped him in a sheet and took him out and buried him." This account goes on to state: "About three hours later his wife came in, not knowing what had happened. Peter asked her, was this the price you and your husband received for your land? Yes, she replied, that was the price. Then Peter said, how could the two of you even think of doing something like this – conspiring together to test the spirit of the Lord? Just outside that door are the young men who buried your husband, and they will carry you out, too. Instantly she fell to the floor and died. When the young men came in and saw that she was dead, they carried her out and buried her beside her husband. Great fear gripped the entire church and all others who heard what had happened" (Acts 5:1-11).

This is one of the most powerful lessons in all of Scripture. This testimony condemns the act of purposeful lying in order to gain power or prestige. Scripture says very bluntly that God hates liars! This is because lying and deceitfulness define the very purpose of Satan who is the enemy of God. What has this got to do with finances? Think back when we considered the relationship between power and money. Power and money are inseparable. By its very nature money represents power in so many ways. It represents the power to give a blessing and the power to withhold that blessing. Money not earned often becomes a curse rather than a blessing.

In the United States of America there are many states that sponsor different types of gambling opportunities such as "Power Ball" and games of chance that promise great pay-outs for a tiny purchase price of one or two dollars. Nobody seems to care that the odds of winning are less than being struck by lightning. These games of chance are very popular since they promise great rewards for little risk. When a certain ticketholder becomes a 'winner', he or she becomes an instant celebrity with more money than a normal person could spend during a lifetime! Recent studies have discovered a pattern in the lives of many of these so-called winners. Many of them have spent their entire winnings in a period of just a few short years. One magazine article featured a man who had purchased a large mansion with a tremendous swimming pool. This article continued the interview with the Lotto winner displaying the beautiful swimming pool, empty and in a state of disrepair. He confessed to being behind in his property taxes and not having the funds to repair or maintain the pool. The article finished by quoting the man saying that he wished he had never won the Lotto in the first place. The article continued showing a number of other such winners who had ended up bankrupt. They simply could not handle such sudden wealth.

In The USA, every wage earner is assessed an income tax on all income earned. This is done on a yearly basis. Each person who is gainfully employed is required to fill out a somewhat detailed form to be submitted to the IRS. Many of the questions asked depend upon the honesty of the wage earner. In some circles it is considered to be a 'badge of honor' if a person can cheat on their taxes and not be caught. Knowing this, the Internal Revenue Service randomly picks out returns that they intend to audit. Sadly, the fear of getting caught is enough to keep some people honest. For a Christian, the concept of "Christ Centered

Finances" demands that the taxpayer be 100% honest in answering all questions on the return. Even if we have the *desire* to cheat, God condemns all such thoughts! It is important to remember that God knows the intent and desires of each person's heart.

CHAPTER 27 JOURNAL

TO CONTROL AND TO DECEIVE

Have you ever used money to control someone else?

How did this work out?

Are you completely honest concerning all of your finances?

List any areas you feel need to be changed.

When do you plan to make these changes?

CHAPTER 28
TO HONOR AND TO BLESS

TO HONOR GOD

Many families have accumulated wealth over one or perhaps several lifetimes. There are times when a family member inherits unexpected wealth. It is especially important during a period such as this that we practice the essence of Christ centered finances. If a family has more than they need, why wait till someone dies? Why not experience the joy of giving to a deserving person, family, or a favorite charity? The amount of the gift is not important. The spirit in which the gift is given is all-important. A pastor friend had been praying for his young teenage granddaughter who was acting out rebellion in her family. She had been in open rebellion which was compounded by an eating disorder. This man had spent many hours praying for his granddaughter. One day, completely unexpected, he received a letter from a church in the town where his granddaughter lived. The letter stated that his granddaughter was raising funds to go on a mission trip to witness to children on an Indian reservation. Realizing that God had answered his prayers abundantly, this man felt led to pour out a blessing on this church. Scripture teaches that if we have freely received, we should freely give.

TO BLESS OTHERS

The power to bless someone may or may not be equated with the desire to bless. The person who has been blessed abundantly may at times become selfish and keep God's blessings to themselves. This is never a wise idea. We should all be wise enough to realize you cannot keep it for yourself. Money selfishly hoarded is like sand running through the fingers and back to where it came from. Scripture clearly teaches it is more blessed to give than to receive. "And I have been a constant example of how you can help those in need by working hard. You should remember the words of the Lord Jesus: 'It is more blessed to give than to receive'" (Acts 20:35). This was spoken by the apostle Paul as he reminded the disciples of the value of hard work and the principle of helping supply the needs of those who worked with him spreading the gospel.

It became glaringly apparent while working as a Development Officer for a Christian ministry, that the ability to give generously often does not equate with the desire to give generously. Those who were tasked with raising funds knew without question that the person wearing a Timex watch was much more likely to be a generous giver than the person wearing a Rolex watch. Many times the rich are far more self-indulgent than the average person. Often when the rich get done meeting their own selfish needs there is very little money left to give to others. Trusting in the words of Jesus it is sad to realize these folks will miss many blessings by not opening their hearts and their pocketbooks to the needs of Christ's ministries.

There was a farmer who over the years became quite rich. When asked how this was consistent with the word of God, he gave the following answer: "Well when I started out God gave me a shovel and I used it to shovel my blessings into God's silo to share with other people. It seems that God also had a shovel and he kept shoveling his blessings into my silo. The only difference was that God had a much bigger shovel." How important it is for us to realize that we can never begin to out-give our Lord. He does not need our gifts since he is the creator and sustainer of our universe. God choses to use us in order to bless others in his name. By doing this God gives us a greater blessing as he uses us to bless others. How important this truth is for every family who desires to have Christ centered finances as part of their testimony.

This author believes in the wisdom of leading by example. His young son Paul, when reading about the need to adopt an orphaned child in another land came to his dad and said, "I want to do that". The minimum amount to give was $20 per month, but this child made only $10 a month from his small paper route. What's a father to do? This author made a deal with his son where together they would support an orphaned child for one year. This little guy proudly brought his $10 to his dad every month and together they sent a $20 monthly contribution to that evangelical ministry. How proud this little guy was when he received a picture of the child he was supporting in a faraway African village. One of the great benefits to our son Paul was that he knew he was doing God's work and he also prayed almost every day for that little boy who he was supporting. His generous spirit also taught his dad a valuable lesson that you cannot out-give our God! Today Paul is a man of God and the father of five, who consistently lives for the Lord. He and his wife have adopted three children into their home. If you are a parent, you cannot begin too early in your child's life to teach him or her by personal example.

CHAPTER 28 JOURNAL

TO HONOR AND TO BLESS

Make a list of ways you can use your finances to honor God.

How many of these have you put in practice?

List ways you can bless others with your finances.

Tell how God has blessed when you accomplished this.

SECTION NINE

Losing Money

CHAPTER 29
LETTING GO OF BELONGINGS

There is a certain group of people sometimes known as 'hoarders' who cannot bear the thought of parting with their possessions. Some of these folks go so far as to fill their house with so much of their so-called 'treasures' that there is little room for people to move around! When her pastor visited one such lady she had to clean off one of the chairs in her living room just so he had a place to sit. With some alarm he noticed that there was a very narrow pathway between each room in her house winding through piles and piles of her accumulated treasures. Most folks would think 'Oh my goodness how sick this must be!' There are several different names for this type of behavior, but there is one root cause. People who behave in this manner have never learned to trust the Lord. Their piles of 'stuff' often represent some sad concept of security. People who hoard money have much the same sickness. During periods of financial disasters people have actually committed suicide rather than face financial ruin. What a sad commentary this is to human values. Scripture offers a simple solution: "And what do you benefit if you gain the whole world but lose your own soul? Is anything worth more than your soul?" (Matthew 16:25 - 26). Another verse states: "So don't worry about these things saying: What will we eat? What will we drink? What will we wear? These things dominate the thoughts of unbelievers, but your heavenly father already knows all your needs. Seek the kingdom of God above all else, and live righteously, and he will give you everything you need" (Matthew 6:31 – 33).

In the fall of 2015 there was a huge forest fire in Lake County, Northern California. This was by far the largest wildfire the state had experienced in a very long time. Hundreds of homes were burned to the ground. Several people lost their lives. There were many millions of dollars in property loss and entire forests were destroyed. Almost immediately television crews descended upon the area, each trying to get the most spectacular story for the evening news. This author watched in fascination as two specific types of responses were given when responding to similar losses. In one town people would be interviewed while weeping as they were devastated by their loss of everything. Within moments the cameras would switch to another family who also had lost everything. But this family was different. These family members were praising God that the entire family had escaped and they were all together once more. This happened again and again with both types of response. Some folks would focus on everything they had lost while others were praising God in spite of their losses. These were the same folks who were reaching out to help others in the midst of their own personal tragedies. Many of these same folks were sharing their Christian testimony in spite of their losses. One woman stated, "I had no insurance but I still have my faith in God." Another man faced the camera and exclaimed, "Thank God we saved little Buster." The camera showed little Buster as being a tiny dog tucked under the man's arm. One entire town was joining together to help rebuild a church that had been destroyed in the fire. God often uses catastrophic events to bring out the best in his people in order to further his kingdom.

Throughout life there are many times and many different reasons that a family may suffer sudden loss. A gentleman in our town was forced to move into a house with another simply because he has lost everything through no fault of his own. It seems his wife had contracted a rare form of cancer and was expected to live for just a short time. The fact was she had lived for several more years. By the time his wife had died this man had lost everything, including his home and his retirement income. He literally had become homeless. There is no family who can ever plan for such a tragic loss, however we all have a choice how we will handle such an event if it were to happen.

Going back to the age-old question, do you own your possessions or do your belongings own you? I urge you to go through your 'stuff' and take a hard look at anything you have not used or needed over the last year. Then ask yourself "Why am I keeping this?" Do I know of a family who could use this more effectively than we are? Is there a charitable organization that can benefit from some of my stuff? How many families rent storage units to keep the possessions that they may not ever need again? Could these extra possessions be sold and the money used for the benefit of God? Is the rental fee, for the storage unit that is storing things we no longer need, a good use of the finances God has entrusted to us? Hmmm…, something to ponder here don't you think? How much of God's money is your family wasting? Every family wishing to have Christ centered finances must begin with the realization that this money is not ours, instead it belongs to God. Our finances have been entrusted to us by God. Don't you think that God expects us to use *His* finances for the common good of *His* people?

Recently the evening news showed another type of sudden loss. After heavy rains, the hillside above a group of homes became a mudslide that partially buried several houses. The force was so intense that houses were lifted off their foundations. Several were declared to be total losses. Two gentlemen, who were neighbors in adjoining, mud-covered houses, were interviewed on camera. It became apparent that one of these men was blaming God for all the rain which destroyed his house, while the other gentleman was thanking God that no one lost their lives. Which gentlemen had a philosophy of Christ-centeredness?

There was a similar situation in California recently where high waves eroded a seaside cliff and several houses literally tumbled into the ocean. Again there were two different responses shown on the newscast. One family was devastated that they lost everything and appeared quite angry. The other family accepted blame for building on the cliff so close to the ocean. The man of the house was quoted as saying, "I should have known better than to build this close to the ocean." Both families had suffered substantial loss. The difference between the two was how they responded to their loss. The focus of Christ centered finances must always be that God owns everything and I own nothing. With this thought in mind, I can never out give God since everything I am giving him he already owns! This ought to take the financial monkey off the back of every Christian! Satan tries to place the monkey on your back while Jesus gently removes it!

What about sudden losses due to earthquakes, tornadoes and floods? Or the sudden loss of a loved one. Which of my 'possessions' are really mine to claim? Answer is, none!

CHAPTER 29 JOURNAL

LETTING GO OF BELONGINGS

What possessions am I holding tightly on to?

Why is this? What's my purpose?

Am I ready to let go?

When will I start this process?

Do I feel guilty for holding on?

Remember that 'guilt' is a gift from the devil. Guilt is a gift which keeps on giving… Better to let go!

Ask God for his grace to let go of guilt and to let go of extra possessions.

Write down the freedom you felt when you became obedient in this area

CHAPTER 30
STARTING OVER

The mind set and heart condition necessary to start over invariably has to come from God. It is so easy to be discouraged and want to quit. But that's the natural answer not the God given way to approach disasters. There is part of a song that comes to mind from someplace out of the clouds, and from many years ago: "Pack up your troubles in your old kitbag and smile boys that's the style. What's the use of worrying, it never was worthwhile, so, pack up your troubles in your old kitbag and smile, smile, smile" This may sound a little 'corny' but it does get the message across. After suffering a tragedy, each person has the choice whether to sink or swim. Put another way, we can learn to fish or sit on the riverbank and cut bait. We can sit and mope or work and hope! Like most everything else in life, this becomes a personal choice with lifelong consequences.

The concept of Christ centered finances becomes very real after suffering a major financial loss. Some families may play the blame game. Others might go into a frenzied panic! Wise families may decide that here is a perfect opportunity for all family members to sit down together and formulate a plan of how the family can survive and prosper in the midst of a financial crisis. No one said it will be easy, but it can be done. Even though it may never happen to you, it pays to be ready. This is somewhat like carrying a spare tire just in case you get a flat. The Boy Scouts of America have a motto: "Be prepared"! This concept is both practical and vital when suffering a life-changing financial crises. In the real world, be prepared, might involve having your individual escape bag filled and ready. It could involve having an emergency supply of food, clothing, and other life-sustaining essentials. Perhaps the most important single factor will be your mind set. Much like the little engine in the children's storybook. As he was going up the hill he puffed, "I think I can, I think I can". When he reached the top of the grade he ran down the hill shouting "I knew I could!, I knew I could!" This just goes to show us that success is mostly realized in our brain and in our heart.

Another very serious challenge comes to a family when the principal wage earner becomes incapacitated in some way and can no longer provide for the financial welfare of the family. This situation can become critical in a hurry. Here is where wise planning becomes so important. While learning to live within the framework of a written budget, it is imperative that the wise family begins to build a savings nest-egg for just such an occasion. Rule number one, don't panic. Rule number two, pray like you never have prayed before. Rule number three is to forget your pride and begin to ask others for help. Helping other people who are in need is one of the basic tenets of our Christian faith.

When Jesus was asked, "Who is my neighbor?", He responded with the following story:

"A Jewish man was traveling from Jerusalem down to Jericho, and he was attacked by bandits. They stripped him of his clothes, beat him up, and left him half dead beside the road. By chance a priest came along. But when he saw the man lying there, he crossed to the other side of the road and passed him by. A Temple assistant walked over and looked at him lying there, but he also passed by on the other side. Then a despised Samaritan came along, and when he saw the man, he felt compassion for him. Going over to him, the Samaritan soothed his wounds with olive oil and wine and bandaged them. Then he put the man on his own donkey and took him to an inn, where he took care of him. The next day he handed the innkeeper two silver coins, telling him, 'Take care of this man. If his bill runs higher than this, I'll pay you the next time I'm here.'"

Here is a perfect example of how God expects each of us to act toward our fellow man.

No matter what has caused a financial crisis it pays to remember that this is merely a financial crisis. This does not need to translate into a family crisis. A family-crises happens only when the family unit is in disarray. As long as the family unit sticks together, works together, and most importantly prays together, they can depend upon God to honor their efforts while they are working together to solve the problem. No matter how big the problem may seem at first. There is nothing too big for God! I mean, golly gee, isn't this the same God who created the universe? Isn't this the same God who causes the sun to rise in the East and set in the West every single day? When rebuilding after a financial crisis simply remember this; your family already knows how to build a Christ centered financial plan. Your family should be way ahead of the learning curve since you have done it once already. Simply formulate your plan, down on your knees, while rolling up your shirtsleeves and starting to work! The hero in a Western movie once exclaimed to his girlfriend, "What the heck, we've made and lost seven fortunes in our lives, this one can't be no different". This same concept should apply to each of us, no matter what the crises. The mind set and heart condition is what really matters.

CHAPTER 30 JOURNAL

STARTING OVER

Start at the beginning, what is my beginning point?

If I have experienced a great loss, am I still feeling sorry for my loss?

When will this stop?

How much control do I have?

What are my choices?

SECTION TEN

Look To The Future

CHAPTER 31

PLANNING TO RETIRE

If you are reading this book and are still intestate, meaning you have not yet written your will, put down the book, collect your thoughts and your spouse, and together start writing down what you want to have happen when you die. I believe it to be inexcusable and downright selfish for a man or woman to die without leaving a will behind! Just recently in the USA a well-known and fabulously wealthy singer dropped dead at the age of 50-something without leaving behind his last will and testament. What a terrible mess he left behind! The news media had a field day! There was conjecture of a love child, who could become the sole heir to his considerable fortune. Many other so-called 'relatives' seemed to literally come out of the woodwork to claim their portion of the prize! Yes, he died suddenly of unknown causes, but this seems hardly to be an excuse for not planning ahead. Here he was, dead, with no ability to direct the dividing up of his estate. Hopefully you will learn from this tragic tale and get your will finalized and recorded in a timely manner. Some folks don't like to talk about or acknowledge the fact that they are going to die! This does not change the fact one tiny bit. You are going to die! It's a fact. We all are going to die! We just don't know when, or where, or how. But the fact is, it is going to happen! Ready or not here it comes! So for pity's sake quit your procrastinating and write you will. I'm certain you have been told that denial (de-Nile) is not just a river in Egypt. (That was a joke). When we consider getting ready to retire what else should be on our bucket list?

WHERE SHALL WE RETIRE TO?

Assuming you have planned well for your retirement, you are now in the position to settle wherever you wish. For many folks this becomes the question of how close we wish to live to our children and grandchildren. Do we wish to leave behind old friends? How attached are we to our present house? Is it our home or just a house? Do we envision moving as a hopeless chore or an exciting adventure? Next we need to examine the cost of living in various locations. The climate is always important, especially if we are moving from or into extreme climatic conditions. Am I constantly freezing or does too much heat make me want to pass out? If I am married, how much do I wish to consider the desires of my spouse? Oh my goodness gracious, how many decisions must we make? Many of us absolutely hate to make long-term decisions. If this causes undue stress why not just stay where you are and vegetate? Conversely you may wish to become like the pioneers of the wild West, in the United States. You may just load your wagon, buy four mules then join a wagon train and head west. "Westward Ho the wagons"!

CHAPTER 31 JOURNAL

PLANNING TO RETIRE

Are you one of those rare individuals who has everything thought out and written down long before that special day when you plan to retire? If so, congratulations! If not, read on!

Why do I need to plan?

When do I need to start this process?

Let's be honest, what is holding me back?

Make a list of things I fear about retiring.

Try to write down what the fear is all about.

Start giving your fears to God in prayer, one at a time.

Finally, don't forget to thank God for taking your fears away

CHAPTER 32

TAKING STOCK OF RESOURCES

For many middle-class families the equity in your home is by far your greatest financial resource. If you have been living in the same home for a considerable length of time, your house may already be bought and paid for! What a huge relief this is! For many families, this is not the case. However, your equity, the difference between the value of your home and how much you still owe on your mortgage, is a significant financial asset as you plan to go into retirement. How does this asset become available for use during retirement?

REFINANCE THE EXISTING MORTGAGE

At the time of this writing, in the USA and throughout much of the industrialized world interest rates are at or near zero! This creates an unbelievable opportunity for homeowners to consider refinancing their home at a greatly reduced interest rate. This, in turn, has the potential to reduce the monthly payments on your mortgage by several hundreds of dollars per month! This certainly merits our attention as we prepare for retirement. Simply stop and think for a moment how much more you could do to benefit your local church and the overall kingdom of the Lord, if you had several hundred extra dollars per month, tax free! This is so easy to accomplish! It's really a 'no-brainer'. Your only out of pocket expense might be a small charge to assess the current value of your home. Your only limitation might be if you have a low credit score. Your credit score is very important! This is a good time to remind you of the importance of raising your credit score!

REVERSE MORTGAGE

Another possibility might be to investigate the opportunity to refinance your home with a reverse mortgage contract. Extreme caution is advised here. Just like there are many tics on a hound dog, so there are many forms of reverse mortgages. The basic premise is that you maintain the present cash value of your home and the mortgage company gains all of the future appreciation of your home. In return, the mortgage company pays you in cash for all the equity you own in your home. If your home is not paid for, this type of mortgage can also eliminate all future monthly payments on the home! In some states in the USA there is a clause in the agreement that the surviving owner must remain in their home throughout their life. There may be also other clauses which limit the amount of time that a house may be 'up for sale' after the death of one party. It is strongly suggested that an attorney be involved in any such transaction. Preferably an attorney who specializes in real estate transactions. The small amount you pay may save considerable expense and frustration in the future. Hire a good lawyer!

OUTRIGHT SALE

It should go without saying that the simplest way to gain access to your equity is to sell your home. If you choose to do this beware of the taxman! In the USA you will be assessed a capital gains tax on any appreciation of your home beginning with the date of purchase. This could be a very large amount. Current IRS law states that this capital gains tax may be avoided and rolled over into the future if you purchase another home within one year. I believe your new home needs to be more expensive than the one you sell for this tax benefit to incur. Again, consult with an attorney who specializes in real estate law.

OTHER RESOURCES

Downsizing your home and other possessions can be a significant act freeing up additional resources. Many couples entering retirement age recognize the fact that more is not necessarily better. A smaller house with a smaller yard may look quite attractive. This could mean less house to keep clean and less lawn to mow. Automobiles are another source to consider. Two people certainly do not require a seven passenger van that was necessary when the kids were at home. You may decide that two cars are no longer needed. This can free up considerable resources including smaller insurance bills.

There are many other potential resources for you to consider as you prepare for retirement. Retirement annuities paid by employers or unions as well as your own IRA's and all other investments need to be examined. The cash value of whole life insurance policies is another source of retirement income. Wisdom would dictate not using the cash value of your life insurance policy unless absolutely necessary. You bought the life insurance to benefit your loved ones after you die, not necessarily to spend on yourself. Finally, there is the possibility in the USA that Social Security benefits may still be a reality. Who knows, stranger things have happened!

Social Security benefits should never be expected to cover all of your costs of living in retirement. These funds may, however, add a little 'frosting to your cake'. Then again, you may not like frosting. You may not like cake! You may not feel right about accepting any government money! If this is your feeling, why not accept your checks and sign them over to your local church. That way, wasteful government spending can be used to build the kingdom of God! Enough of this! Since I'm feeling a little 'goofy', it's time to take a much-needed break.

CHAPTER 32 JOURNAL

TAKING STOCK OF RESOURCES

Making a list. Take your time, try to include everything.

Checking it twice, making sure to include my spouse! He or she may remember assets that have completely slipped my mind! Make sure not to overlook savings bonds and other investments.

CHAPTER 33

FINDING PEACE WITH GOD

As we approach the eventuality of retirement, many new emotions come into play. Sadly, many folks of retirement age are not at all comfortable with the thought of retirement. Emotions span the spectrum of anxiety to boredom and everything in between. One fear for many folks approaching retirement age concerns maintaining their present standard of living. What if my money runs out? Or what if our cash or currency is devalued by the government? Or how much should I worry about inflation? What new activities do I contemplate during retirement? Will the necessary funds be there to finance these activities? Then comes the big question of our health. Many times questions are raised concerning future health needs. These are all important, valid concerns. For us older folks, the cost of medications alone is staggering! With this said, let's read on.

Remember the title of this book, "Christ Centered Finances"? Please take a few moments to reflect on what this means to you. Is Christ truly in charge of your life? Have you made him Lord of everything? Are you trusting him to meet all of your needs? Look at what Christ has to say on this subject, "So don't worry about having enough food or drink or clothing. Why be like the pagans who are so deeply concerned about these things? Your heavenly father already knows all your needs, and he will give you all you need from day to day if you live for him and make the kingdom of God your primary concern. So don't worry about tomorrow, for tomorrow will bring its own worries. Today's trouble is enough for today" (Matthew 6:31-33).

As I continue on my journey, growing older and older, these words of Christ's become more and more powerful with every passing year. In my younger days I used to ride horses quite a bit. Without fail, when the horse was returning after a trail ride it would pick up its speed when it spotted the barn. The horse new from experience that the barn represented both food and the promise of a long rest. As I look towards heaven and my final rest, all the 'stuff' of the world seems rather unimportant. I invite you to look at life in a similar manner. By getting rid of some of the junk that bogs us down we find a new freedom to live for Christ.

CHAPTER 33 JOURNAL

FINDING PEACE WITH GOD

Jesus gave this promise to his disciples when he knew he was about to leave them: "I am leaving you with a gift – peace of mind and heart. And the peace I give isn't like the peace the world gives, so don't be troubled or afraid. Remember what I told you: I am going away but I will come back to you again. If you really love me, you will be very happy for me, because now I can go to the Father, who is greater than I am. I have told you these things before they happen so that you will believe when they do happen. (John 14:27-29).

Reflect on this fact, that Jesus loves us unconditionally!

What does this mean to you, personally?

How can this change your life today?

How does this help you when looking to the future?

Take time to write down the personal victories you have in Christ.

SECTION ELEVEN

Getting Ready To Go

CHAPTER 34

UPGRADING YOUR WILL

Most wills need to be upgraded or modified from time to time. Situations often change over the years which may dictate the need to periodically address portions of your last will and testament. This being said, I seriously suggest that you set aside a generous period of time when you and your spouse can go over each of your individual Last Will and Testament Documents to make certain that each of these state your present wishes for when you die and can no longer make any adjustments. For most people, several years have passed since these documents were first written. Many events have likely taken place that may well have a bearing on your present wishes and thought processes. There are times when it is best to start over and write new wills. An informed lawyer can help you make these wise decisions

MEETING WITH EXECUTOR OF ESTATE

It is important to make certain that the original person you named as executor of your estate is still alive, and that he or she is still both willing and capable of serving in this capacity following your death. If not, then an addendum needs to be added to the original document naming a new Executor. If this is the case, make certain the newly named executor understands what is involved and accepts this responsibility. If at all possible it is desirable that you meet with the executor to discuss your will in detail. Questions can be asked and your executor will have the opportunity to understand your intent as well as the written instructions. This can be very important. Also make sure that your executor will have access to the document upon your death. You may find it advisable to give your attorney a copy.

MEANINGFUL ASSETS

Many folks find it helpful to divide up and give away meaningful assets before they die. If there are several beneficiaries this can be especially helpful to discuss which articles are meaningful to specific beneficiaries. Things like jewelry, special artifacts and firearms may all be divided long before your death. The last thing you want is for arguments or hurt feelings to take place after you have left the scene! It's so much wiser to divide these things up beforehand.

CHAPTER 34 JOURNAL

UPGRADING YOUR WILL

What decisions can I make today that will make it easier for my loved ones when I pass?

Make a list of your incidental miscellaneous possessions and to whom you wish to leave each item.

If you can bear to part with them, why not give away many of these items to your chosen beneficiaries before you die. They can then enjoy these possessions while you are still around to enjoy their fellowship!

CHAPTER 35
UPGRADING FAMILY DOCUMENTS

POWER OF ATTOURNEY

If you are old enough to retire, you should appoint someone you trust to be given the power of attorney over your affairs, if at some time in the future you are unable or unwilling to handle your own affairs. Under normal circumstances the logical choice would be your spouse. Maybe you are questioning the wisdom or necessity of such a document. In the USA a power of attorney is a document that your next of kin or other person of your choice may find very useful in the event you are no longer able to make a decision concerning who will run your affairs. An example of this could be a sudden disaster such as automobile accident or a massive stroke. The oncoming of Alzheimer's could certainly be another possibility. Without such a document it may be much more difficult for others to understand or follow your wishes.

DURABLE POWER OF ATTOURNEY

In the USA, a durable power of attorney is a legal document signed by you and witnessed by two others which gives a person of your choice the legal right to make health decisions on your behalf at any time when you are unable to make them for yourself. These would include, but are not limited to decisions when to stop life-support attempts to prolong life. Without such a written document, your physician is required to take all possible steps to prolong your life even when you are no longer responsive. Your durable power of attorney will specifically instruct your caregivers whether or not to prolong your life with artificial means. This often removes a heavy burden from loved ones who are in crises because of your physical condition. Let's be honest, it's the right thing to do!

DIRECTIVE FOR HEALTHCARE

In many states in the USA a directive for healthcare is very similar to a durable power of attorney. Either document may be used to protect your caregivers from legal and moral consequences for their actions. If possible, make these tough choices for them while you still are able!

LIVING WILL

In some states in the USA a document called the Living Will may act in conjunction with other documents to accomplish many of the same things as a Directive for Healthcare or a Durable Power of Attorney. As always, if in doubt, it is wise to consult with your attorney.

LIFE INSURANCE

This would be an excellent time to dig out your original life insurance policies and read them over carefully. Pay special attention to whom you have listed as beneficiaries. Is this still your wish today or have things and situations changed? Are all of the beneficiaries named in your policy still alive? Are they still in the position to really benefit as you originally intended? Are there other persons or institutions which you might wish to add? These are family documents that are often overlooked until after the death of the policy owner occurs.

CHAPTER 35 JOURNAL

UPGRADING FAMILY DOCUMENTS

Which of these documents do you currently have?

When was the last time they were updated?

What documents do you need to produce?

Have you given copies to your physician, hospital, and attorney?

CHAPTER 36

PRAYERFUL DECISIONS

As each person prepares to leave this Earth, there are a number of prayerful decisions that need to be made for the benefit of those loved ones we will leave behind.

FINALIZE YOUR 'BUCKET LIST'

There are usually several things a person wants to accomplish before they die. There may be places you truly wish to visit. There may be events you wish to participate in. There may be a crazy experience such as bungee jumping or diving out of an airplane or shooting a class III rapids in your favorite canoe. A former president of the USA decided to skydive on his 90th birthday! You might wish to visit some famous landmark or even to take a cruise. I challenge you to make your bucket list and start to fulfill it while you still can.

SAY GOOD-BY BEFORE YOU DIE!

Are there some folks very dear to you that you want to see before you die? Why not plan to go and visit them? If you can't go to them, perhaps they can come to you. If money is a concern, consider sending them finances necessary to make the trip. After all, do you want to visit with them in person or do you just want them to come to your funeral? Friendship is a powerful force, don't leave this Earth without renewing it with everyone you can.

PLAN YOUR FINAL ARRANGEMENTS

Planning your own funeral arrangements in detail can be one of the most loving gifts you leave behind for your loved ones. Understanding many mixed emotions your survivors will have, why not lift the burden of having to plan your funeral? You can do it without putting a date on the document! If this causes you indigestion, why not meet with your pastor and do the planning together. This will be especially helpful if you give written instructions to the pastor as well as written plans for the service. Specify any special songs or hymns you would like to have included as well as favorite scripture verses. Write out a generous check for the pastor to help pay for his services. (Make sure to sign the check!)

FUNERAL ARRANGEMENTS---WRITTEN

It will also help those you leave behind if you meet with the funeral directors and make the necessary pre-arrangements with them. Write out your instructions whether to cremate or bury your body. Select a casket or urn. You may also wish to purchase a burial plot at this time as well as a headstone or marker. Finally, take out your checkbook and pay for all the services in advance. If you can't afford this now, how will those you leave behind be able to afford it? If you choose to be cremated and scattered at sea or some other location, write these decisions down. When all this business has been concluded make certain that your spouse or next-of-kin has a copy of all documents. If you pay in advance, make certain to receive written receipts since you will not be around to plead your case after the event! This, my friend, represents Christ Centered Finances!

NAKED INTO WORLD AND NAKED LEAVING

"Now godliness with contentment is great gain. For we brought nothing into this world and it is certain we can carry nothing out. So having food and clothing, with these we should be content" (1Timothy 6:6-8).

Quite frankly I hope my wife will bury me in my 'birthday suit' and not waste a finely tailored suit that no one will ever again see! I would much prefer that my clothes be given away to others to enjoy as much as I have enjoyed wearing them.

HEAVEN – BOUND!!   MAKING CERTAIN!!!

Scripture teaches that to be absent from the body is to be present with the Lord. This promise is for all those who have trusted in the sacrifice of Christ upon that cross to pay for their sins. "And this is what God has testified: he has given us eternal life, and this life is in his Son. So whoever has God's Son, has life; whoever does not have his Son does not have life. I write this to you who believe in the Son of God, so that you may know you have eternal life" (1 John 5: 11-13). In the Gospel of John, we read the following: "For

God so loved the world that he gave his only son, so that everyone who believes in him will not perish but have eternal life. God did not send his son into the world to condemn it, but to save it" (John 3:16 -17).

CHAPTER 36 JOURNAL

If these verses are new to you, please find a trusted pastor or Christian friends to help you apply them to your life. You will be eternally glad that you did!

If this book has been useful, I would prayerfully ask you to share it with friends who you

Feel would profit from it as well. The third book in the series,"Things That Matter" is titled,

"CHRIST CENTERED FAMILIES" 'Your Kids Matter' and is due to be released in the fall of 2016.

POSTSCRIPT

The following thoughts from the Book of Proverbs in the Bible are included for your further consideration:

MAKE CERTAIN YOU ARE READY!

> "Don't brag about tomorrow, since you don't know what tomorrow will bring" (Prov.27:1).

WELFARE IS FOR SINGLE WIDOWS AND ORPHANS... ONLY!

> "Those too lazy to plow ...will have no food in the harvest" (Prov.20:4).

POLITICS AND POLITITIONS

> "The wicked take secret bribes to pervert the course of justice" (Prov.17:23).

STRESS GIVES YOU ULCERS

> "A peaceful heart leads to a strong body..." (Prov.14:30a).

YOU CAN'T TAKE IT WITH YOU

> "Don't wear yourself out trying to get rich..." (Prov.23:4).

> "Better a dry crust eaten in peace than a house filled with feasting-and conflict" (Prov.17:1).

> "If you help the poor you are lending to the Lord - and he will repay you" (Prov.19:17).

> "Some are always greedy for more, but the Godly love to give" (Prov.21:26).

And from the Book of Job comes the final thought,

> "…I came naked from my mother's womb, and I will be naked when I leave" (Job 1:21).

Thanks for reading:

"Christ Centered Finances"
'Your Money Matters'
Bill Yeomans

www.ingramcontent.com/pod-product-compliance
Lightning Source LLC
Chambersburg PA
CBHW070854180526
45168CB00005B/1809

* 9 7 8 1 5 1 8 6 9 5 2 3 0 *